Staff Development on a Shoestring:

A How-To-Do-It Manual for Librarians®

Marcia Trotta

HOW-TO-DO-IT MANUALS®

NUMBER 175

Neal-Schuman Publishers, Inc.

New York   London

Published by Neal-Schuman Publishers, Inc.
100 William St., Suite 2004
New York, NY 10038

Printed and bound in the United States of America.

The paper used in this publication meets the minimum requirements of American National Standard for Information Sciences—Permanence of Paper for Printed Library Materials, ANSI Z39.48-1992.

Library of Congress Cataloging-in-Publication Data

Trotta, Marcia, 1949-
    Staff development on a shoestring : a how-to-do-it manual for librarians / Marcia Trotta.
        p. cm. — (How-to-do-it manuals ; no. 175)
    Includes bibliographical references and index.
    ISBN 978-1-55570-730-9 (alk. paper)
    1. Library employees—In-service training—United States. 2. Librarians—In-service training—United States. 3. Library education (Continuing education)—United States. 4. Public libraries—United States—Personnel management. 5. Career development—United States. I. Title.

Z668.5.T75 2011
023'.8—dc22
                                                                    2010050754

Contents

List of Figures

Preface

Staff Development on a Shoestring: A How-To-Do-It Manual for Librarians offers library managers a one-stop guide to providing ongoing professional development activities using very little money. It concentrates on methods for keeping staff current on cutting-edge procedures, strategies, and technologies to better meet community needs.

Continuing education opportunities are a necessity for every library if employees are going to be in a position to achieve a uniform standard of performance. Our goal is to see that every patron receives the same quality of service whether he or she is there at ten o'clock on a Monday morning or at three o'clock on a Saturday afternoon. We want our staffs to be aware of and competent in the ways to deliver services that meet current patron needs, which may be a combination of new and traditional techniques. The libraries that we walk into today are quite different from those we may have known as children, or from those that operated while we were in college. The past decades have brought incredible changes in how we deliver library services and in the composition of the public to whom we deliver it. These facts alone are indicators that we all could use refresher courses. Each librarian must make the commitment to reach beyond our library's own walls through professional reading, workshops, and conferences. We cannot, however, stop there. Ongoing training is indeed the foundation of staff development. It is a portion of management responsibility that cannot be ignored.

Staff development must also be concerned with the overall personal development of our employees. The atmosphere that we attempt to create for our patrons so that they will enjoy visiting us must be the atmosphere that is developed by the staff. The library must be employee friendly as well as customer friendly. We all spend a large portion of our lives in the workplace, so we should expect to be treated as well as those who are with us for a few minutes of their day. To create a worker-friendly workplace, management must include flexibility in scheduling, a comfortable area in which to take a break, safety and environmental precautions, and an overall concern for staff well-being. Staff will perform better if all members are treated with respect and dignity. This is the true foundation for staff development.

The best way to accomplish good staff training with very little money is to design in-house training programs that turn experienced staff into proficient trainers. *Staff Development on a Shoestring: A How-To-Do-It*

Manual for Librarians provides model programs for the most in-demand development areas, including chapters that showcase some of the best examples of this type of grassroots training effort from libraries across the country. In addition, today's libraries can also take advantage of the many educational opportunities from other disciplines and from other geographic areas without travel or much expense. For the many incredible learning opportunities accessible from within our own libraries, we owe many thanks to modern technology!

Chapter 1 is designed to help you understand the importance of staff development, whatever the available budget. Chapter 2 discusses creating a staff development program and addresses library policies with regard to development. Chapter 3 gets into the meat of the book—in-house training. Chapter 4 continues the in-house training discussion from the managerial side. Chapter 5 presents best practices for in-house training. Chapter 6 discusses mentoring as staff development. Chapter 7 reviews development opportunities outside of your library. Chapter 8 presents several model training programs that can be used as written or adapted for your library. Chapter 9 shows how technology offers easy, no-cost ways of staying current. Chapter 10 discusses how staff evaluations can serve as regular development tools. Chapter 11 looks at ways to reward performance. Finally, Chapter 12 offers a resource directory.

I hope you'll find *Staff Development on a Shoestring: A How-To-Do-It Manual for Librarians* to be a practical guide for libraries that are interested in offering continuing staff development using this grassroots approach. Please duplicate the many forms and handouts and adapt them to your particular situation. I hope this book will set your library on a course of continual self-improvement, training that will surely result in better service to your users.

Stating a Case for Staff Development

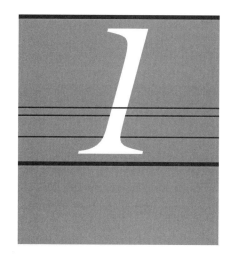

Things change rapidly and often in our profession. Just when we think that we are "cutting edge" and totally up-to-date on new technologies, something else is introduced to the market. It doesn't take too long to realize that with all the training we have, even with our painstakingly earned diplomas from library schools, we have limitations. We quickly realize that we live in a world that requires both ongoing learning and acquisition of new skills. The community outside of the library walls is a changing one, and this is the world that the librarian must know, in addition to knowing the latest developments that make libraries work efficiently.

As professionals, librarians have been committed to the process of continuing education for many years. The professional literature overflows with reports on how important it is to build on our previously acquired knowledge, skills, and attitudes. To refresh our basic education, we are faithful attendees of workshops, seminars, and conferences. If librarians are to maintain high standards, we agree that continuing education is essential. We recognize the need to master new concepts and methods, and often we need to pursue new skills for specialization within a specific area of our discipline. For the library to be recognized as an indispensable agency in the community, the library staff must be energetic and competent. While this "out of the building" method of continued learning has long been recognized as both valuable and appropriate, it should not be considered as the only way of keeping our staff current. Even in the best of times, other ways should be investigated. Not only might other methods be more cost-effective, but they will vary in the content offered and in the means by which staff members learn.

Staff Development Defined

Staff development is the ongoing process that orients, trains, and teaches, through a systematic approach, members of the library organization to work together to serve its customers. It can also reshape attitudes and help staff members become aware of current relevant trends. It keeps staff members in communication with one another and helps them become aware of how their behavior affects the overall library operation.

Staff development is not one thing, but rather a combination of many different types of opportunities that allow staff members to grow. These include continuing education, specialized training, and general personal growth and professional improvement. Staff development includes a broad range of activities that address improving the career needs of both support and professional staff. These development activities can be position related or career related. They may address the quality of life in the workplace or provide a means of personal enrichment. Their commonality is that they will help nurture a staff so that its members are more productive, more efficient, and more effective.

Staff development does not have to be complicated or costly. In fact, a relatively easy step in the process can be taken when staff members are given time to read, think, and plan on the job. It sounds simple, yet, when pressed for time or short-staffed, librarians are often shortchanged of these simple tasks. The library director can facilitate staff development by encouraging staff members to write articles for newsletters, starting with the library's own, or for local outlets such as the Chamber of Commerce or local press, or for professional journals. This is professional development in that the writers must organize their thoughts and document a project or method that is being used. In addition, staff members' confidence in their skills might increase as they share their knowledge with others.

Staff meetings are also excellent ways to encourage professional development, if those meetings go beyond the routine "housekeeping" sort that act mainly as a communications tool. Directors can develop agendas that encourage studying what other libraries and librarians are doing, or even arranging to visit them. Staff exchanges between libraries bring new ideas, new practices, and new outlooks with very little expense, but with great practical gains.

Discussing community and national issues also facilitates professional development. To be a true community resource, it is important that staff members are aware of and knowledgeable about these current issues.

All of the aforementioned considerations fall under the umbrella of staff development. This book touches briefly on many of these components of staff development but focuses mainly on training, a specific form of education aimed at developing skills.

Better Service through Staff Development

Library boards and directors share the responsibility of providing ongoing staff development, so it is important that funds be designated for continuing education workshops. Equally important is the commitment to allow staff the in-house time to participate. The library board sets library hours; if it is evident that closing the library for a morning or a day will make a difference in service, the board's policy should allow for this.

REASONS TO OFFER STAFF DEVELOPMENT

- Improve professional practice.
- Retain employees who are learning and growing.
- Maintain and improve employee skills and competence.
- Keep abreast of new technologies and practice.
- Comply with professional standards.
- Boost employee morale.
- Improve patron satisfaction.

The library's patrons will understand as long as they are given adequate notice so that they can plan for their library needs, and they are sure to be happy about being served by a well-trained staff. The director has the responsibility of bringing the development needs to the attention of the board, and of convincing them of the necessity of development, so that they will approve the required time and funds.

In developing the mission and goals of the library, the library administration must realize that it does not exist in a vacuum. It is a major part of the management's responsibility to examine how the library fits into the overall community that it serves. How does its goal correspond to the goals of other organizations or departments within an academic atmosphere (such as Literacy Volunteers, United Way, Chamber of Commerce, strategic planning committees, or curriculum committees), and how can the library work with any of these cooperatively? Library management has a responsibility to determine how its services can be part of the solution to the problems its community is facing. Libraries have tremendous potential. It is important to realize that potential.

As a profession, we need to broaden our vision of what public library services can mean to the "community" and what impact these services can have on society as a whole. Consider, for instance, story hour at the library. The children who attend these programs develop language, listening, and social skills, and learn how to ask questions. These skills stay with them as they face new experiences and opportunities. Although the librarian who led a particular story hour may not realize it for years to come, if ever, this situation may prove to be a significant example of how the library can affect people's lives. Furthermore, consider the impact that this experience has had on the adult caregiver or teacher who has brought the child to the library. Did they pick up some new skills to share with the child for whom they are responsible? Did they borrow library materials to take home to read to the child? Was their career impacted by the example of the librarian? Or consider the librarian who reintroduces the use of the library to incoming freshmen. These individuals may not have used library research services before, or if they have, many have used only general sources. Imagine the impact the librarian can have on their studies as they learn of specialty collections and databases that will support their majors. Our staffs need to be equipped with the best training possible to make this kind of impact and to be fully aware of what library services could and should be. This will lead to staff members providing better services to patrons.

Improved Core Competencies

Every librarian who has a master's degree from an American Library Association (ALA)–accredited program in library science and information studies should meet the basic requirements that are listed in the ALA's "Core Competencies of Librarianship" (available at http://www.ala.org). This document, which was approved by the ALA Council on January 27, 2009, is divided into individual sections that address basic areas of library work and can be useful when evaluating a staff's training needs. These are the main areas of core competencies, which can be expanded into a training goals checklist that details the specific staff skills that you wish to develop:

1. Foundations of the profession
2. Information resources
3. Organization of recorded knowledge and information
4. Technological knowledge and skills
5. Reference and user services
6. Research
7. Continuing education and lifelong learning
8. Administration and management

For more information on developing a training goal outline, see Choosing a Training Topic in Chapter 2.

Costs versus Benefits

Although it is true that ignoring staff development can cost the library money in the long run, it is also true that providing development does involve costs. How can a library afford to offer training opportunities to the staff when money is a limited resource?

There is never enough money in a library's budget to do all that is needed. However, if a library is to succeed and grow, staff development must be included in the budget. It is essential to the overall delivery of service. Central to the policies that guide any service organization should be the issues that relate to human resources. We should be investing a tremendous amount of effort in human resources because people are the prime component of delivering good service. But how can we accomplish this with the limited resources that libraries and most other nonprofit organizations have at their disposal?

The amount of time and money allocated to staff development will vary from library to library, depending on resources. The two major cost areas involved in staff development are staff time devoted to the process and the cost of any materials that may be used. Some programs can cost hundreds or thousands of dollars; some can be implemented with no monetary cost at all. What we must recognize is that even when programs are free, some cost is always involved, as you will need to invest staff time in the program.

For example, if the library has chosen to use one of its staff members for training (one form of staff development), the training time plus preparation time must be factored into the cost. Remember, also, to factor in the time needed to implement the changes and to follow up with feedback.

Alternatively, if outside trainers are used, the library must consider the cost of their fees as well as the salaries of the staff members participating.

For example, consider the following two sample scenarios of costs related to a staff development program:

Scenario I: Outside Trainer

Cost of the trainer	$500
10 staff members @ $30/hour for 2 hours	$600
Training materials	$100
Cost for this method	$1,200

Scenario II: Staff Member as Trainer

4 hours preparation time @ $35	$140
2-hour training session @ $35	$70
10 staff members @ $30/hour for 2 hours	$600
Materials	$100
Cost for this method	$910

You can use the blank worksheet provided in Figure 1.1 to calculate costs associated with your training program.

Figure 1.1. Cost Analysis Worksheet

	Description	Cost
Salaries/Wages		
Fringe Benefits		
Consultants		
Travel		
Materials and Supplies		
Equipment		
Other Costs/Fees		
Indirect Costs/Overheads		
TOTAL PROGRAM COSTS		

What is the cost of not providing training? While the dollar costs are saved up front, the long-term cost may be far greater. Staff who are untrained are more likely to provide poor service. Poor service may reflect on the library's image. A poor image may result in negative public relations, and eventually decreased funding.

All organizations pay for training, regardless of whether they intend to do so. Not having a structured program in place means that your organization pays for training day by day on the job in a way that makes it more costly and inefficient. It is much better and more economical to have an efficient training program in place. Investing time and money in training will have great payoffs for you over the years. It will reduce the time that it takes people to get up to speed, and reduce the likelihood of mistakes.

Staff Development as Continuing Education

Libraries are recognized as centers for lifelong learning. The services libraries offer provide users the opportunity to continue their learning in ways that surpass the traditional boundaries of education. Why, then, have we consistently turned toward the traditional methods of education for our own development? Why not take advantage of methods that the new technologies make possible? Why not utilize our own skills for the provision of development?

Workshops, seminars, and conferences are valid means of providing educational opportunities that will enhance staff development. This book is not intended to discourage anyone from participating in them. However, we should selectively choose what will suit our particular library best, rather than worrying that we will miss something if we don't attend all of the workshops. These programs often require substantial registration fees and travel expenses, and those might make such programs prohibitive. The issue becomes even more complicated because most libraries do not have enough staff members to send some to workshops and have others cover their assigned tasks. Thus, the challenge is to find alternative ways to have all staff members involved in continuing education because the effective delivery of library services is dependent on all library personnel being competent all of the time.

Staff development should be offered to each and every staff member. In doing so, we recognize that the staff contributes greatly to the library's successes and failures. Certainly, the collection and the facility are important. Perhaps more important, however, is service; our goal is excellent delivery of that service. The staff's performance in the workplace and its attitudes toward that workplace stay with all of the members as they assume their roles in the community. Ultimately, this is what will determine the overall success of the library. Although the director sets the goals of the library, the staff carries out the tasks to achieve those goals. Therefore, each and every staff member must be a good spokesperson for the library. Shared staff development can help foster this.

REASONS TO OFFER IN-HOUSE PROGRAMS

- Boost morale.
- Increase efficiency.
- Provide a comfortable learning environment for staff.
- Provide skill development that can be used in daily work.
- Save staff time for travel.
- Reduce costs associated with training.
- Provide opportunities for in-depth discussions among all staff.
- Encourage staff to enlist the support of their colleagues to provide better service.

It is not an option to forgo the process with the excuse that we "just don't have the money." This book presents possible solutions to providing ongoing, inexpensive staff development to supplement the formal process. It is based on successful experiences. Because we depend upon our staff members to perform productively, efficiently, and accurately, we must have the assurance that they are always on the cutting edge. Library directors and boards should commit to providing opportunities for staff members to update their knowledge and skills, as well as to providing approaches for them to meet new challenges and to develop as individuals. Our hiring processes should always include questions that help determine the prospective employees' attitudes toward this idea of professional development, and their responsibility toward their own development.

Creating a Staff Development Program

Libraries, by their very nature, are labor-intensive organizations. While we depend upon our resources, it is even more important to have staff who are able to perform the most essential function: matching the information resources to the needs of the individual user. If staff members are going to be able to do this, they must be highly productive and motivated. A thorough staff development program is a key component in motivating the people within your organization to become advocates for it. Orientations, staff meetings, readings of professional materials, workshops, lectures, electronic delivery methods, and formal course work are all important components of a staff development program.

To design a staff development program that will bring out the best in your staff, the library must have a clear idea of its training philosophy. What the library administration perceives to be important is what will guide the design of the development program.

Library Policy and Staff Development

The performance of a library lies within the ability of the staff to deliver the best possible experience to patrons. As the world continues to change, and as technology continues to evolve, it is important to keep library staff on a path of continuous learning through staff development training. This training should not only expand staff members' knowledge; it also should relate to the goals of the library's customer service policy (see sample policy in Figure 2.1).

It is the responsibility of the library's governing authority to set the policy for the organization's staff development with the input of the director. While some members of the board may not be sure of its importance, the director has the responsibility to emphasize what impact ignoring the process might have. A good staff development policy will incorporate the positive effect that ongoing staff development has on the staff, and ultimately on service. It may include information on how often a staff member may participate; it might also encourage participation in

---

Figure 2.1. Sample Customer Service Policy

Customer Service Policy
Anytown Library

The Anytown Library strives to offer excellent library services to all. In addition to the quality of the facility and the collection, it is equally important that the library staff provide accurate, efficient, and friendly service at all times. Although we often view the patrons as the clientele, it is important to remember that the patron, as a voter, taxpayer, tuition payer, etc. (whatever is appropriate for the type of library), is also the ultimate boss.

The customer service policy is the foundation for all staff interactions with the general public. All other library policies should be interpreted in light of the principles outlined below:

1. The library should offer the same quality of service to all regardless of age, race, sex, nationality, educational background, physical limitations, or any other criteria that may be the source of discrimination.

2. Patrons should be treated as if they are the most important people in the world. They are!

3. Judgment calls should always be made in the patron's favor; mistakes should always be to the patron's advantage. Staff will not be penalized for errors made in good-faith pursuit of this policy.

4. Patrons should never be left without an alternative if a staff member is unable to comply with their request.

5. Staff members should be familiar with and able to articulate library policies as well as explain the rationale behind them.

ADMINISTRATIVE ROLES IN STAFF DEVELOPMENT

- People in authority make the decisions about the purpose and the means for staff development.
- The board has a responsibility to see that the staff has not only knowledge and skills but also professional and personal growth.
- The board and the director must be visible, vocal, and persistent advocates of staff development.

professional reading and membership in professional organizations. Some organizations may even include the membership dues as part of the staff's professional development benefit.

Figure 2.2 presents a sample staff development policy. Please note that it is intended to be just that—a sample. Every library is unique, and we should not simply take policies from other libraries and call them our own. Rather, samples should be the basis of ideas that evolve to meet the specific needs of our own libraries.

Determining Responsibility for Staff Development

Many large companies and even some libraries have a staff member whose position (e.g., the director of human resources) includes the responsibility of overseeing staff development within the organization. Many libraries cannot afford to pay someone to fill such a position, so the responsibility falls upon the shoulders of someone who may not have been specifically educated in staff development. In my experience, I have found that the responsibility for staff development often goes to the assistant director or to department managers. Each library will have to determine what staffing configuration is right for its particular situation. In any case, the duties of whoever is responsible for coordinating staff development will be very similar from library to library. The staff development coordinator will find it necessary to follow the planning

Figure 2.2. Sample Staff Development Policy

Staff Development Policy
Anytown Library

Anytown Library is committed to creating a workplace that:

- acknowledges the key principles of feedback, growth, and accountability;
- enables the continuous learning of staff;
- enables staff members to reach their potential by offering career development opportunities;
- ensures that staff is appropriately skilled to meet patron needs; and
- encourages and recognizes staff for work-related achievement.

To support these commitments, Anytown Library facilitates the ongoing training and development of its staff. As such, staff members will be compensated for the dues required to be part of the state's professional organization. Each staff member will be required to participate in a minimum of two hours of staff development activity per month under the supervision of the library director. These activities include, but are not limited to, attendance at meetings and workshops, professional readings, and online webinars.

process, from the needs assessment to the feedback and evaluation components.

Assessing Your Library's Needs

The planning for staff development begins with the identification of specific issues of education and training within the library. A needs assessment process, very similar to that used for evaluating library service to the community, is necessary to develop a program that will be truly responsive to the needs of both the organization and the employees. Discover what the employees think they need. Determine what the organization thinks the employees need to know to have a successful library.

There is no one "right way" to conduct a needs assessment; several methods can be used. The director can, of course, use formal survey tools. While these may seem somewhat impersonal, they can give a very thorough picture of training needs. Informal discussion with staff is also an appropriate way to gather training needs. (For more on formal and informal survey tools, see Chapter 3, pp. 23–24.) The director might also use the performance appraisal/review process as another way to develop a list of training programs. Staff should be encouraged to identify gaps in their knowledge, experience, and competency that might potentially affect their ability to perform at a high standard at their job.

The staff development administrator will also have to determine who will be trained. Is it one or two people? Is it the entire staff? Ideally, all staff should have access to any development opportunity that they feel might be useful. Realistically, we know that this is not possible in most cases. Therefore, the administrator must set priorities. Obviously, setting reasonable limitations is one of the ways in which the library director can control some of the costs of ongoing development.

Designing a Development Program

As a next step in the planning process, the library's management will have to make some essential decisions before staff development begins. First and foremost, the library should ensure that its program is visionary, looking toward the future while keeping an eye on present needs. Management should design the program to have the following characteristics:

- The program goals must be achievable.
- The program should be flexible enough to encompass new ideas, to explore new developments and trends in the field, and to accommodate adaptation.
- The program should establish the library's direction for growth and services, clearly and specifically.
- The program must relate closely to the library's goals and objectives.

A program capable of doing this will be driven by those priorities which reflect users' needs. Management should seek input from the staff for the planning process. This type of overall plan for staff development will result in a more organized and comprehensive program. It will provide all of the staff members a broader perspective on the library as a whole, as well as show how their particular positions fit into the whole scheme of library service.

Several factors will influence the outcome of a staff development program and are therefore key considerations in the program's design. Administrators must consider not only the acquisition of new skills but also the preservation of institutional memory: How are longtime employees passing on their accumulated knowledge to newer colleagues? This commitment must be passed on from the top to all staff. The person organizing the program for the library must know the capabilities of the group and time restrictions: What will staff members be capable of learning in a given period of time? How much time can the library spend on any given staff development program during a given year? The amount of time allotted is tied directly to results. Most staff developers would agree that the goal of staff development is to increase individuals' knowledge, understanding, and skills as well as to change behaviors and values.

The overall plan for staff development is the most crucial element in determining whether you will have an organized, purposeful program in place. It is an investment of time that will have tremendous payoff. The planning process helps determine the long-term vision of the library, and it helps identify ways to fulfill goals. The staff development program at your library should be in a continuous closed loop that perpetuates a healthy growing entity. Not only will there be fewer problems in a workplace that has a built-in nurturing system, but the employees will

WHY MANAGERS SHOULD PROMOTE STAFF DEVELOPMENT

- Managers are better able to assess the competency of their staffs.
- Staff development can function as a motivational tool.
- Shared responsibility for staff development can help identify and train new leaders.
- Shared training opportunities build and strengthen team performance.
- Staff development programs help staff members become as effective as they can be.

be better able to relate their everyday work tasks to the underlying goals and objectives of the library.

Choosing a Training Topic

The best topic to choose for training involves areas of service that need improvement in the institution's approach to customers and potential customers. These needs should have been identified during the assessment process (see earlier section). The list of possible topics appropriate for training workshops that is presented here is by no means all-inclusive but will help to get your library thinking about possible course selections.

After the selection of the topic, the next step is to use the appropriate resources to complete the training outline (see Figure 2.3). This tool provides a preparation checklist that will prompt the trainer to complete all the details as he or she develops the plan.

The library's overall commitment to continuing staff development and the needs assessment process will determine how many programs the library should offer, how often to offer them, and their length. These are the types of details that can be determined only within each library.

Getting Staff On Board

Library staff members have limited time to participate in learning because of their many responsibilities. They must view time spent in any sort of development as a worthwhile investment if they are going to participate. Even if the development activity is mandated by management, participants will not keep an open mind unless they view the process as valuable. In addition, the pressures of normal day-to-day tasks can limit attention spans. This should be considered when deciding what time of day the programs are offered, as well as the length of the sessions.

To maximize motivation, staff members must be made to believe that what they learn will increase their effectiveness, add to their professional skills, and enhance the skills that they already have. Job satisfaction is realized in people who have an investment in their training; this consideration helps create a good psychological foundation for the entire learning process. It is helpful for individuals to be able to see the impact of their learning on job performance; this helps them get in the proper frame of mind to learn. People want to be recognized as valuable to an organization, and they want to know that they have made contributions to it and are, in fact, shareholders in its success.

Internal Marketing

At one time or another, we have all received important information through the grapevine. It's never a good thing. We all know how

TRAINING TOPICS

- Collecting Oral Histories
- Communicating Effectively
- Creating Good Impressions
- Crisis Training
- Customer Service
- Dealing with Angry Patrons
- Dealing with Conflicting Personalities
- Developing Intergenerational Family Programming
- Effective Building Management
- Getting There: Goal Setting
- Getting Things Done
- Humor in the Workplace
- Intercampus Cooperation
- Maintaining Equipment
- Managing Capable People
- Managing Collections
- Managing Your Time
- Multicultural Service
- New Technologies
- Organizing Family History Days
- Orientation for New Employees
- People Problems in Public Service
- Personal Development
- Relationships with Friends Groups
- Relationships with Colleagues
- Relationships with Trustees
- Safety, Security, and Sensibility
- Self-Esteem Development
- Stress Management
- Teamwork
- Using Facebook
- Using Informed Judgment
- Web-Based Instruction
- Working Smart
- Working with Volunteers

Figure 2.3. Sample Staff Development Training Outline

Training Topic (Title or subject):

Training Target (Who are you training? How many?):

Training Time (Length of the program):

Training Objective (What is the intended result?):

I. (Broad Content Area)

   A. (Heading):

      1. (Subheading):   Training techniques:

         a. (Topic):   Training aids needed:

         b. (Topic):

      2. (Subheading):   Training techniques:

         a. (Topic):   Training aids needed:

         b. (Topic):

   B. (Heading)

      1. (Subheading):   Training techniques:

         a. (Topic):   Training aids needed:

         b. (Topic):

      2. (Subheading):   Training techniques:

         a. (Topic):   Training aids needed:

         b. (Topic):

(Continued)

Figure 2.3. Sample Staff Development Training Outline *(Continued)*

II. (Broad Content Area)

    A. (Heading):

        1. (Subheading):   Training techniques:

           a. (Topic):   Training aids needed:

           b. (Topic):

        2. (Subheading):   Training techniques:

           a. (Topic):   Training aids needed:

           b. (Topic):

    B. (Heading)

        1. (Subheading):   Training techniques:

           a. (Topic):   Training aids needed:

           b. (Topic):

        2. (Subheading):   Training techniques:

           a. (Topic):   Training aids needed:

           b. (Topic):

Training Technique (What methods will you use?):

Training Aids (What will you use—laptop, whiteboard, overhead projector?):

Training Setup (What will the room setup be [e.g., round-tables that facilitate face-to-face discussions among participants]?):

Other Needs:

information changes when it comes secondhand. If we were to ask our employees how they would prefer to hear important information, I guarantee that the grapevine would rank as their least favorite method. Employees want to be valued and trusted, so they want to receive information from their supervisors—their personal connection with authority. Depending on the importance of the information, employees also like to receive e-mails, newsletters, and memos. Good communication from the top tier of administration to the lowest tier on the employee scale helps overcome the inevitable "who knew first" and "nobody told me" syndromes, and creates a sense of belonging among all members of a library's staff.

If great library service is the "product" that we want our staffs to deliver, then the basis of building this is solid internal communications. It may sound obvious that staff members need to be aware of staff development opportunities to take advantage of them, but too often the communications step is overlooked. An internal marketing program— the organized and deliberate dissemination of information—helps lay the foundation for the staff development philosophy. Internal marketing has results when it is approached by an administration in a manner that demonstrates its pride in the organization and in its commitment to excellence. Internal marketing includes the communication of corporate culture and goals, mission and vision statements, as well as personnel policies and procedures. Internal marketing can also involve initiatives such as informing the staff about new database or equipment introductions or other new acquisitions to the library.

Library management can learn the importance of internal marketing by examining the procedures of America's most successful companies, such as the Disney Corporation and General Electric. These are examples of corporate giants who learned that to be successful with customers they first had to build successful staffs. Internal marketing plans comprise several components, which will be discussed later. The emphasis on these components will vary from library to library, but they are the critical foundation on which a staff development program will be built.

One of the thematic model programs presented in Chapter 8 is a communications module. So often we undervalue this basic human need and fail to recognize that a weak input and feedback system is detrimental to an organization. Every organization has its grapevine through which information is disseminated, but as in that old-fashioned children's game of telephone, as the information travels from one person to another on the grapevine, it changes, maybe due to lack of understanding or, to shorten the story, because individual emotions come into play. Internal marketing cannot depend on the grapevine method if it is to reach everyone with the same message. Rather, a combined system of information dissemination is preferred. Personal contacts, small group meetings, a bulletin board, broadcasting e-mails, blogs, or an employee newsletter will all be useful in developing a strong communications network for internal marketing.

Personal contacts are the number-one method of developing an internal marketing plan and beginning the process of personalizing the workplace. Absolutely nothing will work better for a manager than knowing his or her employees as people. Through sincere concern and understanding of employees' needs, a manager will begin to develop a relationship with the staff. The building of loyalty to the organization will result from the efforts to implement changes to meet these needs and by management exhibiting respect for the staff's abilities.

Internal marketing will set the stage for your staff development program if you invest some time in planning your approach thoroughly, and if you follow the plan consistently. This will link the employees to the organization's mission and create a sense of pride and achievement for all. A sense of ownership results when employees have been encouraged to be creative and contribute ideas, especially when their input has been valued and when feedback has been provided. Employees must know what the library's mission is and why it is so expressed. Only then can they be expected to be enthusiastic about supporting it.

All managers in every type of library want to have customer-friendly organizations. Libraries, after all, are service organizations. We all want to project a positive image to our customers, and we devote time and resources to publicity campaigns (including brochures, logos, bookmarks) to achieve this. A library's value should not be measured by the number of items it holds, but rather by the number of successful customer transactions. It is important to recognize that for libraries to have a favorable image in our communities, we must first have a core culture of good service internally. To achieve this, we must invest both our time and our efforts into building the messengers, the staff members. People, not things, are what make or break an organization. It is therefore reasonable to expect that we should develop thorough, organized, internal marketing programs before we go to great lengths to publicize our library services externally.

Our employees are our image. They are our best, and unfortunately in some cases our worst, advertisements. The library's internal marketing program is necessary for communicating purposes but is even more important for the commitment and pride that staff members develop for their organization when they have a thorough understanding of what their library is all about. They need to be aware of its mission; they must become believers in it. Once this happens, they are likely to become spokespersons for it. Internal marketing makes employees feel valued. The result is that the library becomes a nicer place to work and, it follows, a nicer place to visit.

For an internal marketing program to be effective, staff members must believe that they are part of an organization that is doing good things. Positive actions influence others more than any number of words, and people will reciprocate with positive actions of their own. For employees to make a commitment to action, they must be convinced that they are working for a good cause. They are then able to visualize what library service could be. Staff can develop this vision if they are participants in developing not only the library's goals but also the plan of action necessary to reach those goals. This is the essence of people power, which comes from the administration's sharing its authority with individuals they have come to value for their constancy, their reliability, and their integrity.

ADVANTAGES OF INTERNAL MARKETING

- As libraries empower staff to build stronger customer relationships, internal marketing will provide the drive for greater involvement, commitment, and understanding.
- In difficult times, changes within the organization can weaken the bond between the employer and the employee. Internal marketing can bring the parties together with shared goals and values.
- Internal marketing helps the process of knowledge development by building understanding and commitment.

Homegrown Training

We often assume that staff development occurs only in formal learning situations. This is a rather limited view. Many everyday situations lend themselves to effective teaching and learning. When staff members vocalize thoughts and ideas, they can initiate in-house, or "homegrown," training. A casual discussion with one of your staff members can provide an opportunity to reinforce a certain organizational value, clarify a question about a particular assignment, or suggest a specific resource that may be helpful. A library that is committed to providing ongoing staff development will take advantage of these situations as they arise. Keeping training within the library, among only employees, can be an excellent way to foster staff development.

The library director or staff development coordinator needs to make a personal commitment to each employee who is going to realize potential within the organization. Finding out about employees' interests, values, and aspirations, as well as inquiring about particular areas in which they want to improve, will set the pace for the development program. Staff members' accomplishments are a measure of the successful leadership of the organization.

Developing an In-House Team

One of the best ways to initiate homegrown training is to take advantage of the various talents possessed by your own staff by engaging employees in the training program. You have the opportunity to develop a training network in which all members have a responsibility to succeed because they are invested in the organization's mission to develop interpersonal skills. Sharing the responsibility for training also encourages staff members to be creative and to move toward helping the library accomplish its goals—a motivation that will keep staff members focused.

To develop a network of staff trainers and support systems from among your employees, you must empower them. Empowering employees does not mean dumping all of the grunt work on them. Rather, it refers to the delegation of both authority and decision making, a sharing of power between leaders and employees. The process of empowerment is dependent upon vision, resources, and the employees' ability to make decisions. Library managers who are good leaders will see the value in this. Leadership means getting things done through people, and empowerment is key to utilizing our staffs as part of the internal training network. Thus, activity that supports this empowerment makes the employees believe (and rightly so) that they are being enabled to act rather than being manipulated. This process in itself will become a long-range motivator for staff members.

The effective library director or manager will be able to build a team of people who work collaboratively to achieve a common goal. This team is not found in organizational charts, but rather in the actual functions that team members perform. Many times, team members "cross" departments; this is an asset, as it strengthens understanding of other people's roles in the organization. Such efforts will produce a staff that will be consistently productive for a long time.

Selecting a Trainer

The manner of presentation is critically important in determining the overall success of a workshop, so the trainer should exhibit desirable knowledge and be comfortable as well as knowledgeable in providing training. Attributes of effective trainers include the ability to be tactful, calm, and open-minded. They should also be authoritative enough to inspire confidence, trust, and respect. Good trainers are able to be objective, adaptable to a variety of situations, and enthusiastic. They are able to cope with the unexpected and even turn a difficult situation into a positive learning experience. The training process is one of teaching and communicating, so it is important to create a good psychological foundation for it. Trainers must be ready to control the process to provide the broadest possible perspective on the course material.

Library directors and staff development coordinators who are well aware of their staff's abilities will be able to sense which staff members may be ready to begin this in-house training process. Although it is important to provide many staff members the opportunity to offer workshops, you should begin your program with the most experienced people. A good start is very important to the long-range success of your staff training. The staff members who participate in these early successes will be the best advertisement for the programs. If they feel that they are valuable and that their time is well spent, they will carry that message to their colleagues and encourage them to participate as well. Unfortunately, the same is true if they are unhappy with the program. So, to be sure, put tremendous effort into offering a quality program from the very beginning. An effective trainer possesses the following qualities:

- Tactful, calm, and natural
- Open-minded and knowledgeable regarding the subject
- Authoritative enough to inspire confidence, trust, and respect

- Able to analyze accurately
- A quick thinker
- Objective, impersonal, and unbiased in thinking
- Able to stay on track
- Organized, yet flexible to a given situation
- Able to accept information and ideas from others
- Enthusiastic
- Has a sense of humor
- Knowledgeable about human nature
- Patient with the various manifestations of human behavior

Only a "superperson" would possess all of these attributes, so do not be discouraged if no one on staff fits this description. The key to helping any one of them develop into a good trainer is that the staff development coordinator assumes the attributes that may be lacking. At the same time, the staff development coordinator should point out the trainer's strengths and help him or her use those strengths to his or her best advantage. It is also quite possible to pair two employees so that they can "team teach" a workshop. This enables coordinators to draw on their different personalities and abilities in order to find the right mix of leadership for a particular training program.

One of the roadblocks that the staff development coordinator will inevitably encounter is the hesitancy of staff members to become trainers. Many of them will tell you they don't think they are qualified for this type of task. The staff development coordinator's role is to change that thinking. Perhaps this can be the model workshop that the library director or the staff development coordinator offers. Being part of a system that encourages positive self-image is incredibly helpful to staff members. This type of program is a way for them to develop their own skills, as well as appreciate others' skills. The reluctance that many individuals have about participating in homegrown types of programs stems from

GOOD TRAINERS...

- are task oriented. They are able to accept responsibility, and they are adaptable to change.
- are able to challenge people by making them work hard to achieve their goals.
- are expert in their field, and they are able to relate to other subject areas.
- keep their cool in difficult circumstances. They are patient and interested in the participants' needs.
- use a variety of training methods and techniques to help students learn quickly and effectively.
- are enthusiastic, firm yet fair, able to admit they are wrong, and have a good sense of humor.

the belief that they can learn nothing from their coworkers and their coworkers can learn nothing from them. This is not true. The more presentations and workshops I lead, the more I realize how much I learn and benefit from the people I am training. Regardless of the position we hold in the library, we all can and do benefit from other people's perspectives and techniques if we keep our minds open.

To develop individual potential within your library, you must influence the thinking of your group and perhaps sell them on a particular idea, point of view, or attitude. Without a doubt, the following minimums must be met by the training design and by the selection of a trainer for the library to achieve its purpose: Presenters must be knowledgeable. The better prepared they are, the more they are able to instill a sense of confidence in the group. Knowledge breeds confidence. It is important for presenters to be themselves; being natural helps make people most effective. Never pretend to know an answer when you don't. Honesty is better, and people will respect you more if you admit that you don't know but you are willing to find out and get back to them.

Tasks of the Trainer

Once the library has indicated its expectations, the trainer takes on the responsibility of developing or gathering the course materials. Two types of resource materials should be included in developing the content of training sessions. Naturally, most of the materials utilized are specifically designed with librarians in mind; they should include print and electronic sources. The use of these types of resources helps make the learning situations appropriate to our particular library staff members. We must remember, however, that we should be using external resources as well. These are materials that are not strictly related to libraries, and that is actually their greatest value. Borrowing proven techniques and strategies from other organizations prevents us from constantly reinventing the wheel. In addition to being an incredible time-saver, this is a wonderful way of integrating libraries into the mainstream and bringing useful methods and concepts from the mainstream into library thinking. Other agencies will begin to recognize the similarities of our organizations' needs with their own and will have a better understanding of our missions.

The framework for the training program is developed in the program outline, which includes the learning objective(s). The broad context area of this objective proceeds in the outline from simple to more complex concepts. This will help you progress through the course in an organized fashion, and will ensure that important issues are not overlooked.

Because trainers must address so many needs, they should use as many methods as possible to create an environment conducive to adult learning. The physical setting of the program as well as courtesies, such as having coffee available, should be considered in the workshop design phase. The learning environment is enhanced when participants are comfortable and satisfied. The trainer should take into consideration air quality, temperature, and seating arrangements.

Another important aspect of developing a quality training session is creating a sense of continuity. This can be accomplished by a repetition of the salient points throughout the program so that they are reinforced. Each time one of the points is repeated, more information can be given so that comprehension grows sequentially. Substantive presentations can also be enlivened with humor and with interesting language. While we do not intend to present a show, we do want people to enjoy learning. Using humor when appropriate often serves to make the point memorable.

After receiving the overall directions from the staff development coordinator, the trainer has the responsibility to determine the material that will be covered in the session(s); the length of time necessary to teach the material; which training methods will be the most effective; and to develop any handouts, visuals, and bibliographies that will be used during the program. (In addition to the trainer's fee, other cost factors to consider, other than staff time, are printing for handouts, perhaps a manual or text, and refreshments.)

Once you have selected your trainer, your next step will be to determine the library's training needs. You can have a program with terrific content, but if that content is not relevant to your staff, the program is not very helpful to your organization's goals. The expertise and the reputation of the trainer are also factors. If the trainer's style clashes with the staff's needs, the trainer's expertise will not matter.

Determining Training Needs

Training needs can be determined by finding what is currently being done by each staff member and matching that information with what could or should be done, and then establishing priorities. The gap between these two factors will provide you with clues as to the type and amount of training that is needed within your library. This assessment can be accomplished by using a combination of techniques. It is important to understand that no one method alone will provide all the information necessary to determine the library's training needs. Several methods of assessing needs exist.

Surveys are written questionnaires that provide a list of questions. They can be delivered to each staff member in paper format, or, if staff members are computer-savvy, they can be sent electronically. In some cases, the same form is good for everyone. In other cases, managers may need to use one and front-line staff another. In any case, the questions should be brief, specific, and phrased in a way that demands a short answer. It is a good idea to conduct a survey at least twice a year. In this way, the surveys will point out improvements that have occurred as the result of the training and they will also uncover any new training needs. The speed with which our profession has been changing dictates a need for these frequent assessments.

Letters, memos, and suggestions from customers are great sources of information to determine training needs. If patrons take the time to point out something that went wrong, or right, it's not trivial. Requests

POINTS TO REMEMBER

It is important for trainers to keep the following in mind so they will be inspired and able to motivate others.

- When all is said and done, for what do you want the training to be remembered?
- Individuals must accept responsibility for their own development.
- You, as the trainer, can assist others to gain skills and knowledge, but you cannot make them learn. The focus must come from within.
- Keep an open mind when you are training. Helping others develop is one of the ways that we can continue to develop ourselves.

and complaints should be taken seriously. Read between the lines; often what the writer of a note is complaining about is not the entire need, but the symptom of another problem. Equally important are commendations. If something good is happening, try to make it a regular part of the routine at your library.

Minutes from departmental meetings often mention issues relevant to those departments. Read them thoroughly to determine the attitudes they convey. Use this information in training workshops to help achieve staff development goals.

Plans of action for departments convey lots of information. Do the library's different departments have formal, written goals and objectives? Are departments meeting these goals? Are other departments aware of the goals their colleagues are setting? How does one department impact another? These plans are a good source to determine what supportive training the staff will need to carry out projected activities.

Interviews are clearly structured information-gathering tools. Formal one-on-one meetings or small-group meetings are excellent ways to assess learning needs. Be prepared for these. Write down a few questions that require more than a yes or no answer. Write down the responses. Be prepared to listen as well as to ask questions because you are indeed listening for people to tell you what they need or want.

Informal talks will give you a good deal of information. You can have these talks in any setting. Consider what you hear in the coffee break area, the hallways, and the parking lot. Valuable clues abound, and, again, you may need to "read between the lines" as well as to listen to casual comments about personalities and situations.

Simple observations can provide a wealth of information. Become a subscriber to the "walk around" school of management. Keeping an eye on the library during the course of the day is valuable when collecting data. Record key observations when you get back to your desk so you do not forget them.

ACTIVITIES FOR ASSESSING TRAINING NEEDS

A variety of activities are useful in determining training needs.

Formal Methods

- **Survey**: The survey is an excellent way to determine what your library is or is not doing.
- **Letters, memos, and suggestions**: Requests and complaints should be taken seriously. This is a great source to determine training needs.
- **Departmental meeting minutes**: Read them thoroughly to determine the attitudes that they convey.
- **Plans of action**: Plans are a good source to determine what supportive training the staff will need to carry out projected activities.
- **Interviews**: Formal one-on-one meetings or small-group meetings are excellent ways to assess learning needs.

Informal Methods

- **Informal talks**: You can have these talks in any setting.
- **Observations**: Record key observations so you do not forget them.

Writing Meaningful Objectives

As in any learning situation, staff development programs will be most effective when they are developed around a set of learning objectives. To develop these objectives, trainers must consider which competency they want to improve in the staff, and the overall desired outcome of the training session. Then they must take in four essential components in writing the objectives: audience, behavior, condition, and degree. It is absolutely essential that trainers address the participants: Who are they, and what do they already know? Then they must consider behavior: What is the intended observed result? Condition refers to any specific situation that may apply (e.g., the library has been challenged to add new technologies in the upcoming year, and they must determine what they need, how much it will cost, and what the funding source is). Finally, degree addresses how well the learner must perform in order to be considered proficient.

The staff development coordinator and the trainer should compare thoughts on these four components before the final objective is written. Also, keeping in mind that many types of learning exist, they should review Bloom's Taxonomy. First published in 1956, Benjamin Bloom's

BLOOM'S TAXONOMY OF EDUCATIONAL OBJECTIVES

Cognitive

- **Knowledge**: Recalls data or information
- **Comprehension**: Understands meaning of instructions and problems
- **Applications**: Uses a concept in a new situation; apply learning to workplace
- **Analysis**: Distinguishes between facts and references
- **Synthesis**: Puts parts together to create a whole, with emphasis on a new meaning
- **Evaluation**: Makes judgments about the value of ideas or materials

Affective

- **Receiving phenomena**: Awareness, and willing to hear
- **Responding to phenomena**: Active participation
- **Valuing**: The worth or value a person attaches to a particular object, behavior
- **Organization**: Organizing different values; resolving conflicts
- **Internalizing values**: Value system that controls behaviors; pervasive, consistent, predictable

Psychomotor

- **Set**: Readiness to act
- **Guided responses**: Early stages in learning a complex skill that include imitation, trial and error
- **Mechanism**: Learned responses become habit and are performed with some confidence and proficiency
- **Complex overt response**: Skillful performance of motor acts
- **Adaptation**: Skills are well-developed, and a person can modify and use in different situations
- **Origination**: Creating new movement patterns; creativity combined with highly developed skills

Source: http://www.nwlink.com.

The Taxonomy of Educational Objectives, the Classification of Educational Goals (published by David McKay Co., Inc.) is an industry standard in writing learning objectives. This divides educational objectives into three different categories, based on the learning style: The affective domain is how people react emotionally; cognitive objectives revolve around knowledge and comprehension; and psychomotor describes the skills needed to physically manipulate a tool or an instrument. Using a combination of these three will help the trainer write broader objectives that will encompass more learning styles.

Other Training Considerations

Your library could hire an outside professional trainer or speaker, but it is often more rewarding and more cost-effective to find current staff members who can train the rest of the staff. This is appropriate when an individual has special knowledge or experience, or has taken a class or done special training and is, therefore, able to teach staff what he or she has learned. Whichever choice you make, professional or staff member, the following considerations apply.

The Director and his or her management team should determine the learning objectives, which will be used to establish a list of what skills must be learned in a particular training session, so participants know what to expect. These should be presented at the beginning of the workshop for several reasons. First, you will have a way to measure results because you will be able to compare the post-workshop skills with the entry-level skills. Second, the presenter or trainer will have a clear understanding of what is expected in each of the sessions. You should give participants a form stating these objectives at the start of the series. This action will help underline the objectives, and alert participants to what the administration expects of them. These learning objectives do not necessarily summarize the workshop, but sharing them sets the tone, and facilitates learning.

The manager must clearly understand and state in writing the purpose of the training. This must be clear to the trainer and to the staff that will be trained. The library director and the trainer must have an agreement or contract that specifically states what is expected of each party. This agreement should take into consideration the training methods as well as the overall program design. The library director must make a commitment that goes beyond the training process to the application of the newly learned skills. Appropriate and sufficient time to apply these skills must be planned for and then supervised. Last, but certainly not least, is the function of evaluation. This closes the loop and gives the library director the opportunity to see whether the learning has taken hold and is being used or whether further or different training opportunities should be considered.

The trainer must have a professional attitude, credibility, and organizational skills. The trainer should consider some variation of method within the presentation, such as the use of audiovisual materials for visual learners, role-playing, brainstorming, and participatory activities for the audience. This is the performance standard that you want your staff to exhibit in the workplace at the conclusion of the training. The development and the statement of the objective will help the trainer develop the necessary materials for the workshop, decide what method of presentation to use, and design an evaluation procedure so the library will be able to determine whether the training was successful.

The program design is what will ultimately determine learning success, since this is the vehicle for the delivery of the message that you want your staff to receive. It will be structured consistently through the progression of the workshop so that the learning objectives will be achieved. For this to happen, a program must be implemented for the right reasons, using the learning methods that will hold the participants' interest while involving them in the learning process. Program design must be clearly related to participant and institutional needs.

Successful learning is accomplished when the participants are able to relate new materials to a familiar context. It is easier to comprehend something if the learning is intended to be an expansion of a preexisting knowledge base. If the topic is totally new, then the training designs will have to present a truly coherent overview of the materials and then relate the presentations to past experiences as often as possible. It will also be necessary to project how the new skills will improve job performance.

Common Methods of Program Delivery

Once you have selected a trainer, and determined the library's needs and objectives, you must choose a method to design and deliver your training program. Time, group size, and environmental considerations must all be part of the information used to develop the program design. Trainers should be expected to shape the content of the workshop to meet the learning objectives, and this knowledge will assist them in adapting a "generic" presentation to one that specifically meets the needs of your library. Methods of program delivery are numerous, and are discussed in the following paragraphs.

Presentations

At first, some staff members will be hesitant to do a presentation. They may have never spoken before a group, and they may not have the confidence in their own abilities to do the presentation. They also may feel that they do not have any skills that are different from their colleagues, and that therefore their colleagues can't learn from them. However, as the coordinator, it is your responsibility to explain that their presentation is one in a series of ongoing presentations and that other staff members will have their opportunity to share their expertise. You should also remind them that they will be speaking to colleagues, perhaps even friends, and this will benefit the entire staff. One of the very best ways to convince other staff members to join the training network is by showing them how to do a presentation by example. The staff development coordinator and the library director should be the individuals that begin the training program. The workshop that they offer should exhibit a strong personal belief in the program. It should also demonstrate that management values the staff, as they are investing time and effort in training them. In addition, this initial workshop should demonstrate the various training methods and techniques that other employees can incorporate in the training workshops they offer.

When developing a presentation, the trainers should take several factors into consideration. The first item to consider is presence. Body movements, including positioning at a podium, moving through an audience, using hands to emphasize points, and especially making eye contact, are techniques that not only put the presenter at ease, but also serve to draw the audience into the performance. Voice is also an important tool for the presenter. The more variety in pitch, volume, and tempo, the more likely it is the presenter will hold the audience's attention. The length of the presentation must be considered; it should be long enough to cover the subject and short enough to keep it interesting. Content should include both the whys and the hows of the program. The emphasis should be on the how, but the rationale is important too. After all, the "why" is the reason for the workshop.

In the planning of a presentation, the trainer should always set aside time for questions and answers. The trainer should not be intimidated by negative questions; these will almost always be asked, especially when a procedural change is proposed. If the trainer has done his or her homework, and is prepared for the workshop, he or she will be able to counter any negative comments with facts. Usually, the positive questions and comments will outweigh the negative. Those who are truly interested in the topic will bring forth great discussion. And, because all of the members participating already know one another, the recognized personality differences will account for the negative attitude that some individuals may demonstrate.

E-learning

Electronic learning, or e-learning, is the commonly used term used for web-based distance education, with no face-to-face interaction. This is often a cost-effective way to deliver training opportunities to employees. The lessons are generally designed to guide the participant through the course at their own pace. Some of these are timed, while others are not. Many include proficiency modules. With information-based content, no specific skills are learned. The user is provided information that he or she might not have come across elsewhere. With performance-based content, the lessons build on a procedural skill in which the learner is expected to increase proficiency. E-learning opportunities are very useful for libraries to use for staff development. First of all, because they take place in a virtual environment, the participants can take advantage of these based on the library's schedule. They are also cost-effective, as they do not incur any travel expenses. Many of them have practice tests and worksheets that reinforce the information delivered. E-learning makes it possible to have quality learning experiences that are affordable. Most libraries, and even library associations, cannot afford to bring in *the* expert to provide the training that they want for their staff. Many programs allow instructors of the highest caliber to share their expertise. E-learning makes it possible to receive training, often at minimal cost and at a time and place that is convenient.

Chapter 12's Resource Directory will provide some specific suggestions to check for learning opportunities. On a general note, it is important that the staff development coordinator research these to ensure the sites are user-friendly and affordable, and have a reputation of success with learners. Most e-learning companies employ a variety of strategies to deliver their product. These include blogs, collaborative software, e-portfolios, and virtual classrooms. One of the most recent trends in the e-learning world is screencasting. This is the process of making videos available online for viewers to watch. This method has the advantage of giving the presenter the ability to show the flow of his or her thoughts rather than simply explaining them in text. With the combination of audio and video, the expert can somewhat replicate the classroom experience. This is the next best thing to face-to-face learning. Also, from the learners' point of view, this method enables them to work at his or her own pace, and to watch the broadcast (lesson) multiple times.

Audiovisual Aids

We are continually bombarded with multimedia messages, and many people have become used to them, finding presentations without the use of visual aids difficult to follow and even boring. Good trainers must keep in mind that people have different learning styles, and before they design their program, they need to know about their audience. Not every training program warrants the use of audiovisual aids. Trainers should consider several factors. First, what is the trainer's comfort level with audiovisuals? Second, does the subject matter warrant the use of this media? Third, does the library have the technology available to use during the presentation? If the trainer decides to use an audiovisual approach, many types of commercial media are available. However, it is also not difficult to add a video clip of your library, a selection from the Internet, or some other prop to break up the presentation. The following are some suggestions to help trainers use audiovisuals in their workshops.

- Use large charts, slides, overlays, or other media projected onto a large screen.
- Use color to distinguish categories or to highlight.
- Be selective with pictures and drawings, as they require some interpretation.
- Key features should occupy at least one-half of the screen, chart, or display. Do not include secondary details as the visual becomes too "busy" and hard to interpret.

- Maintain eye contact with your audience, even when using visuals, or you will lose them.

- Parallel your flow of words with the flow of visuals. Disjointed concepts can be confusing.

- Flip charts support spoken presentations and let the audience participate as they silently read the copy you have prepared.

- Don't forget about the usefulness of an overhead projector. You can add information to the prepared slides by marking them with special markers.

- Use sound (music, sound effects, and professional voices) for additional impact.

- Prerecorded messages eliminate stammers, stutters, and wasted time. They maintain a level of enthusiasm and zest throughout the performance because they have been edited, unlike live presentations. They are especially useful when you want to extract a message or a quote from a famous person.

- Taped presentations have the advantage of conveying your message exactly the same way each time it is shown. It is a versatile medium because it combines the elements of good communications (movement, color, language, sound, and often music). These can be uploaded to websites and viewed at the viewer's convenience.

- Remember the basic rule: Keep it simple!

Audiovisual aids are training tools, and with today's modern technology can be more useful than ever before. Staff can view them when they have the time, and this method also allows individuals to participate without having to travel. Nevertheless, you should not forget the importance of the carefully planned live presentation. The limitation of taped presentations is that the staff is not able to interact with the presenter unless it is an interactive broadcast done with web cameras so both groups can see one another.

Developing Successful In-House Training

We get better at tasks the more we practice them. Staff training is like anything else. The more often we offer training, the better we become at anticipating the needs of our staffs, providing good training workshops, and projecting the impacts and outcomes of situations. It is important that the administrators and the supervisors of the library take a turn at offering training. Through this they set an example for other staff members.

The following suggestions will assist you in becoming more comfortable with beginning a staff training program within your library. Once you begin, you will no doubt find shortcuts and methods that work well for you and will make the process of training second nature to you. This list will help you whether you are doing the training yourself, are using other staff members, or are turning to outside help.

- Ensure the training the library offers is of high quality. It must project the administration's concerns and professionalism. The quality of training sends a strong message to staff about the quality of the organization.

- Every trainer must have a clear understanding of what the expected outcome of the training is to do a good job.

- Encourage staff members to become trainers. One of the very best ways of mastering a subject is to teach it to someone else.

- Trainers must always remember to be themselves; being anything else is a mistake.

- Trainers must learn to become task competent; that is, they must develop the skills, knowledge, and relevant experience for specific tasks so they can share them with others.

- Trainers must be interpersonally competent. They must be socially skillful, able to sense the feelings of individuals and of the group as a whole, and be personally persuasive.

- Good trainers practice, either in front of a mirror or a small circle of family or friends. Practicing is a part of preparation.

- Practice what you teach. Good trainers are good role models and use the skills that they want others to imitate.

- Make available supportive handouts and resources.

- Use media appropriately to enhance the presentations. Be certain that the equipment is working and that you know how to control it. Never use any material with a group that you yourself have not heard or viewed.

THE RIGHT PEOPLE

- Choose the right people for the jobs; choose action people; interview them to find out what they are really like.

- Assign new staff members to a team at the outset. Brief them on informal rules and customs. Let them know that they are welcome and important to the team.

- Train new staff to achieve immediate results. Share the library's objectives. Find out what newcomers already know. Provide information on how they are doing. Feedback and encouragement are vital!

How to Train Your Staff Members

Employees bring to their workplace and workshops an established set of skills, a body of knowledge, and certain attitudes about work and education that can affect the outcome of the process. It is important to establish an active atmosphere. Provide opportunities for both input and response during the training period. If the session includes a lecture portion, a good strategy to remember is to pause after you present each major idea. Ask the participants how this idea or concept might affect their particular job. This not only clarifies whether they understood the information, but involves the participants. It is always easier to understand new ideas if examples are provided. Examples help the participants incorporate the information presented into their own knowledge base and apply it to their work. Role-playing or practicing a skill in a simulated situation involves participants and reinforces the ideas presented.

From these techniques, you can see that the trainer is maximizing the involvement factor in order to keep the participants focused on the program. Learning is an act of change. If students are resistant to change, they will challenge their need for learning. The trainer can help them minimize their resistance by providing them with positive feedback.

Helping participants understand the meaning of their new knowledge and helping them relate their newly learned skills to real life and already familiar experiences can also be accomplished through question-and-answer sessions. In any event, in this type of skills training, the material presented should be directed toward immediate application. When the information provided applies immediately to one's experiences or background, understanding is increased. The old standby test is: "Is it relevant?" Starting with familiar ideas and concepts creates an environment of relevance and makes participants more receptive to absorbing and integrating new information. All of these strategies will help the library plan a more effective staff development program, because the program design is intended to maximize adult learning. To encourage staff to take full advantage of training sessions, managers should provide suggestions for preparation, participation, and follow-up. Figure 3.1 provides a sample handout for employees.

Starting with an icebreaker is especially helpful if the group includes many new people. This technique is a way to introduce people to one another in a manner that is relaxed and minimizes self-consciousness. A common icebreaker is to pair people and have them share information with each other for three to five minutes. At the end of the allotted time, the partner shares the information that he or she learned about the new

Figure 3.1. Homegrown Training Handout: Getting the Most Out of Training

Before Attending

Discuss with your supervisor what you hope to gain from the training workshop and how it will change your job performance. Think about the problems for which you might find solutions by interacting with other participants.

Some Participation Tips

Much of the success of this program in terms of its usefulness to all participants depends on your attitude. You should do the following:

1. Enter into discussions and talk with other participants.
2. Be willing to learn from the experience.
3. Meet with new people.
4. Search for new ideas.
5. Listen carefully to the subject content.
6. Get involved as much as possible when there are activities.
7. Use time well.
8. Refer to the objectives of the program, and think, "How can I use this in my work?"

After Attending

Talk individually with your supervisor about the training, whether it lived up to your expectations and how you will use your newfound knowledge. Don't be afraid to ask your supervisor for support as you begin to apply these new skills. Your supervisor will check back periodically to see whether you have followed through with what you learned and to determine if further training is necessary.

colleague. This has the benefit of introducing people to one another, but it also sets the tone for the session and allows for some boasting that one probably would not otherwise do. If the group has many new people, a scavenger-hunt type of icebreaker is often helpful. The trainer will have preprinted handouts that ask a variety of generic questions, such as "Where were you born?" and "Do you speak more than one language?" All participants are instructed to visit with each person in the group and ask them at least one of the questions on the list. In most cases, this leads to people chatting with one another, and the trainer will have to "call time" in order to get on with the rest of the session.

Discussion is an important part of both large and small training sessions. It is a very useful technique. Small-group breakouts and brain-storming sessions are specific examples of discussion techniques. These methods are especially useful when library management is interested in having the group formulate a solution to a particular problem. In this type of training session, the trainer actually becomes a facilitator. The questions or cues the facilitator provides should be geared to eliciting ideas from all of the participants. The group should not criticize or dispose of ideas during this process. Respect for all is a key operating factor of this process. They should wait until all ideas are presented, and then evaluate each of them in terms of their practicality as part of the solution. Having the staff evaluate alternative solutions and choose the one that the majority feels is most suitable is a gigantic step toward solving the problem. The group can then move on to determine what other steps are needed to achieve the desired result and, with the facilitator's assistance, assign responsibilities to its members for moving the process forward.

The library management, if it chooses to use this form of training, must clearly spell out what is expected. Management must guarantee the participants in this group process the freedom to implement their plan. The trainer or facilitator should not give his or her own viewpoint, because doing so will have the effect of telling the participants what they should do. The trainer's job is to listen to the discussion and to see that the participants do not lose sight of their purpose. The trainer should also assist the group in summarizing their plans so that they can be implemented. Group members assume ownership of the plan through this process and thus they are committed to following it through to completion.

In some instances, especially when the participants have not had problem-solving experience, it is very useful to employ case studies. Like examples, case studies often have the effect of making the learning situation more relevant to the participant, rather than dealing with broader issues or concepts. A case study is actually a written description of a given situation. It teaches how to analyze the important aspects of how to arrive at conclusions or solutions. In many situations, when interpersonal relationships are at stake, this method will help the staff develop insight. Participants will learn how to separate the relevant facts from those which are not as important. Most crucial of all, the participants will learn through this method that if they communicate with one another, they will be able to see matters from more than one point of

TIPS FOR TRAINING

- The trainer selected is to be viewed as the resource person.
- Adults do not always view themselves as needing to learn, most often because of the responsibilities that they are already carrying. They must be convinced that we all learn from one another.
- Most of the work involves repetitive situations. Planning an exciting, creative way to expand job horizons brings a welcome change to the routine when accepted and integrated into the worker's own style.
- People do things for their own reasons. Motivation to learn cannot be passed onto employees. Rather, it comes when participants are offered learning situations that are relevant to them.

view and therefore will be more flexible in the workplace. Case studies are one of my favorite methods of training, because regardless of the content or the intended outcome, the most important lesson of all—communicating—is learned.

The lecture is an informative presentation, designed to explain an idea or a concept, by the trainer, who has much more knowledge on the subject than the group to be trained. If the group has some basic knowledge of the subject, it is much better to use one of the aforementioned training strategies instead. Lectures can be direct, clear presentations of the facts in a relatively short time frame. They can be accompanied by PowerPoint slides to emphasize the key points. However, if the trainer is not a good speaker, or is not well-prepared, the lecture method can become dull and deadly. My advice would be to use this method sparingly, and when you do use it, choose a trainer who is always well-organized, well-prepared, and able to deliver the material in an interesting way. The right person in the right situation can inspire a group and motivate the desire to learn and do.

The opportunity to practice newly acquired skills provides the repetition and reinforcement that some individuals need to complete their learning. It is also a way for the trainer to evaluate the progress of the participants' skills. Therefore, it makes good sense to have a module for every workshop that allows for the practice of newly obtained skills. This practice reinforces the objectives because the on-the-job application of skills will illustrate the importance of these objectives. In many instances, this practice feeds back to components of the training. This provides a means of observation and measurement of the outcome.

The Manager's Responsibilities for Training

All organizations, whether they are nonprofits, such as libraries, or profit-making businesses, have a tremendous need for an innovative, creative workforce. As an administrator, you must be able to influence others and to shape events and activities within your workplace to achieve the goals of your organization. In general, people are very eager to know what job you want them to do and what standards you have for good performance. People want to succeed, and they become more motivated by success because success builds their confidence and makes them feel competent. People who feel good about themselves are more willing to be proactive and embrace new experiences more readily.

Effective staff development results in lasting and noticeable change in the behavior of staff members. Its value is that it helps us make staff members more productive while using fewer resources. This chapter is intended to provide assistance especially for managers who are responsible for developing, overseeing, and, most important, communicating the need for ongoing staff development to trustees or funding sources.

Starting a new training program can be overwhelming. It is often helpful to talk with colleagues about their experiences: what worked, what did not work, and why. The following pages will assist you in walking through the development stage of programs, through implementing and evaluating them. They are basic and certainly not all-inclusive, and are not intended to be step-by-step guides. They are management techniques that can be applied to staff training programming.

Conveying the Library's Vision

Employees must be able to visualize what library services should be in the future in your community. They can have this vision if they are participants in shaping the library's goals and if they have a part in developing the plans that are necessary to bring the library to these new levels. The resources are both human and inanimate, and they are dependent upon

IN THIS CHAPTER:

✔ Conveying the Library's Vision

✔ How to Accomplish Specific Job Training

✔ Customizing Staff Job Descriptions

✔ Helping Staff Maintain Perspective through Positive Feedback

✔ Keys to Successful Problem Solving

✔ A Manager's Self-Audit: What It Takes to Be a Competent Leader

WHAT MANAGERS SHOULD ASK BEFORE BEGINNING A STAFF DEVELOPMENT PROGRAM

- What do the participants need to know and what must they be able to do?

- What kind of staff development will be most effective in engaging participants in learning?

- What kind of staff development is most likely to cause participants to apply what they learn?

- What evidence will I look for and accept as indicators that the participants are applying what they have learned?

the library's financial support. These resources are the tools the staff needs in order to proceed on the path toward reaching the vision.

Presentation and discussion of the vision is not a one-time event. To be effective, the manager must communicate the vision day in and day out. It should be considered to be a living force in the everyday operation of the library. A good vision is coherent and has the commitment of the staff. It is important to have unity of purpose and ownership of vision, so that staff members can relate the vision to their own values and aspirations, and they can participate through their accomplishments in helping the library achieve this vision.

How to Accomplish Specific Job Training

The following are some examples of what we need to have successful training for specific jobs:

- Give employees clear, dynamic job descriptions.
- Give employees a written statement of performance expectations.
- Concentrate on teaching simple tasks first.
- Break tasks down into components to make them more easily understood and achievable, and less overwhelming.
- Keep teaching cycles short and reinforce the teaching by practice.
- Develop skills through hands-on practice and repetition.
- Develop strengths and capacities into required skills.
- Motivate trainees with motivated trainers.

The nature of libraries is that staff members work best when they work with one another, not in a vacuum. Therefore, it is important for managers to stress team building. This should be the everyday practice, not just a one-time exercise to learn how to be a team. As with any team, the management (coach) devises the game plan and then aids and supports the staff members in carrying out that plan. Here are some ways to support team building among employees:

- Clearly communicate the mission of the library. Your goals determine how you will use the allotted resources.
- Make sure that employees know what the library stands for by providing a statement of values, expressed positively. Write it as you intend to live it; your values govern your day-to-day operational philosophy.
- Encourage rituals and traditions, as these create goodwill and are the ties that bind the employees to the organization and create a sense of unity. Your staff's performance reflects the organization's philosophy.
- Use internal marketing. Your employees' feelings toward the organization for which they work and its policies affects the quality of customer services.

Figure 4.1. Customer Service Training Handout for Managers

Library Philosophy

As a library, we want to provide friendly, responsive, efficient service to all of our users. We will do this by having a caring, respectful, and positive work environment that values all individual talents as we strive to reach our common goal. To achieve this, we continually seek innovative approaches to provide efficient, accurate, and complete information services.

Training Tips

- Distribute official customer service policy.
- Explain how library goals are connected to customer service (see, e.g., Figure 8.11 on p. 79).
- Encourage employees to make informed judgments.
- Help employees maintain a positive attitude.
- Use group discussion activities.

Perhaps the most important thing for staff members to know is the library's mission and/or philosophy. This details what the library is trying to achieve, and sets the standard that employees must meet to do their jobs effectively. Figure 4.1 provides a sample library philosophy and customer service training tips for managers.

Customizing Staff Job Descriptions

Customizing the description of an employee's work will both help us achieve the required results and will also serve to challenge the abilities of the particular staff member who is holding the job. Combining the customized description with training gives the individual the independence and freedom to be innovative and to develop and channel his or her energies and skills to the advantage of the library system. Improvisation and enhancement require mastery of the basics of the job.

In describing positions, we must be able to provide established boundaries while at the same time encourage employees to pursue their strengths. These descriptions are best when they are fluid and adaptable. The following are some important areas that should be included in an attempt to describe tasks:

- **Work functions**: What will the person do?
- **Accountable results**: What will be produced as a result of work over a given period?
- **Strengths**: What are the major abilities that an individual should possess that can be channeled toward achieving intended results?
- **Motivators**: What energies will drive the individual toward the required results?
- **Limitations**: What are unacceptable actions and lines that cannot be crossed?

- **Resources**: What know-how is available; what tools or information sources can an individual use to achieve results?

- **Delegated decisions**: What level of authority has been delegated to the employee to make decisions without checking with someone else?

- **Consultative decisions**: What type of decision must be checked with a supervisor before it can be executed?

- **Prescribed activities**: What tasks *must* the individual perform according to the organization's philosophy?

- **Responsibility potential**: What are the implications for new responsibilities to be assigned (i.e., what is the promotion potential)?

Because results and accountability are of paramount importance, we can see the necessity of continuing staff development and training within our organizations. The focus has shifted to performance and production, and the changing nature of our practice requires that results become every person's responsibility. Periodic assessment of these results sets up the performance review process within the system. Results are what we ultimately will reward and compensate. The following pages are intended to provide some actual, hands-on advice that can be used by the library administrator and passed on to other supervisors and trainers.

Helping Staff Maintain Perspective through Positive Feedback

Library work is very satisfying, but patrons do not always express their gratitude. This can be very disheartening. As the administrator, you need to be the staff's cheerleader. Here are some things you can do to assist the staff in developing a good attitude:

- Make a list of staff accomplishments. Seeing the positive will help staff members realize they can overcome difficulties at work.

- Emphasize that they need to have enough information to see the whole picture, and that you will provide it.

- Point out that blaming others and buck-passing costs a lot of energy, time, and motivation, and it really interferes with progressive action.

- Discourage procrastination by setting reasonable deadlines and standards.

- Teach employees to look at tasks in a series of steps. When tasks are broken down, they are not nearly so overwhelming. Each step accomplished should make those remaining easier.

- Encourage employees to list pluses and minuses of situations; this exercise will help them see situations as they really are.

- Remember that when you stop learning on the job you begin to "shrink." If you are overworked, focus extra motivation on different tasks to keep you growing.

- Create strategies that will help staff deal with pressures rationally.

You can also motivate employees by providing positive feedback on their performance. Even though many people are modest or even suspicious about accepting compliments and praise, it is very important to share positive feedback. Giving praise is a reward for a certain individual or individuals, but it also can be an opportunity to provide on-the-spot staff development. When staff members hear praise for an accomplished colleague, others will be reminded of what is expected of them. The praised staff member sets the standard to which others should aspire. The following are some hints for making your praise most effective:

- Be as specific as you can and explain how the staff member's actions benefit the library.

- Make the praise concise to avoid embarrassing the staff member.

- Do not allow the person to say "it was nothing." Interrupt them (politely, of course) with a smile and say, for example, "Don't try to talk me out of complimenting you!"

- Be sincere.

- Specify what you are recognizing the employee for, rather than using a generic "Great job!"

- Make praise personal and individualized.

- Know when to praise in public and when it is more appropriate to praise privately.

Keys to Successful Problem Solving

Every organization faces problems, some small, some large. Solving the problems, or in some cases, finding alternate methods of accomplishing tasks, are great opportunities to involve staff members. These "learning on the job" situations are also development opportunities. In order to be successful as a manager during difficult times, it is important to keep in mind the following:

- Stay objective.

- Determine what actually happened.

- Ask for suggestions from employees and advice from colleagues.

- Evaluate suggestions and advice and put only the best to use.

- Follow up on results to see whether the solution has solved the problem.

- Be sure to reward good performance, but never poor or non-performance. Be sure all employees have received the message that their performance matters.

ENCOURAGING STAFF

- What do the participants need to know and what must they be able to do?

- Delegate. Share responsibility and authority to get a job done.

- Create opportunities. Encourage your staff members to be partners in change to increase the action orientation of their outlook.

- Understand the staff's prevailing mood. Does this need to change?

- Build consensus. Make sure everyone understands what is going on and why.

- Manage by support and encouragement.

- Lead by inspiring and encouraging others to work for solutions.

- Set the standard for excellence by example.

- Remember that making mistakes means you are taking risks and trying to make intelligent choices. Mistakes are part of the learning process.
- Accept that the best solutions usually take time to come to fruition.

Manager's Self-Audit: What It Takes to Be a Competent Leader

Many individuals are confident when they take a job that they know exactly what they need to do to accomplish their job. Others are less so and often grow into their position through trial and error. Where do you fall? Before we can begin to help others with their self-development, we must be very sure of our own. It is important to assess our own strengths and weaknesses and work out our own plan for improvement. The manager's self-audit will help you assess your abilities and point out areas in which you may need to strengthen skills. These hints should help you avoid some of the pitfalls that can destroy your enthusiasm for a staff training program within your library.

As the administrator, by definition you are the leader, so consider these questions:

- Are you able to have others follow your direction?
- Do you have vision?
- Are you able to innovate, to focus, to rationalize, to make decisions, to handle pressure?
- Are you trustworthy?
- Do you have a sense of humor?
- Do you encourage involvement?
- Are you committed to principles?
- Are you persistent until you accomplish a task?
- Are you the opposite of any of these?

Remember the following as you perform your own self-audit:

1. Leaders are action oriented.
   a. They plan, set priorities, and implement.
   b. They keep things moving.
   c. They are concerned with impact and results rather than with getting bogged down by process; they get the job done.
   d. They are analytical and systematic; they make tough decisions.
2. Some of the skills and characteristics of leaders include:
   a. Self-confidence
   b. The ability to conceptualize and set goals
   c. The ability to communicate well

TIPS FOR ACHIEVING RESULTS AS A MANAGER

- Focus on your goals.
- Keep control without interfering by delegating.
- Choose the right people.
- Challenge people to take on new experiences.
- Don't "dump" jobs on employees.
- Share responsibility and power.
- Delegate gradually.
- Gain commitment by involving people in the process.
- Learn from mistakes.
- Keep employees involved.
- Do things right and do the right thing.
- Set an example that will encourage people to trust and support you.

    d. The ability to manage a group process

    e. Objectivity

    f. The ability to listen to all sides of an issue

    g. Self-control and tolerance

    h. Stamina and good humor

3. Leaders are supervisors.

    a. They accept responsibility and are accountable.

    b. They genuinely want to help others develop.

    c. They are successful when they use their time efficiently to mobilize others to perform.

    d. The best leaders of all are those who are able to help others to outgrow them and become leaders themselves.

Library managers have so many responsibilities and duties. Those who take on the role of being education advocate for their staff will be rewarded with work performed by well-trained individuals. In addition to having a clear understanding of the mission and the vision of the library, staff members who receive training also will be able to understand the principles or guiding beliefs of the organization and then apply them in daily operations. The result will be staff achievements and better service.

The critical part of any training is making employees understand their jobs in the context of the total operation. If managers keep this in mind, they will help their employees understand and believe in their value within the organization. This will lead them and the organization to success.

STEPS TO LEAD YOUR LIBRARY TO SUCCESS

- Be enthusiastic; it is infectious.
- Work hard, but take time to enjoy what you do.
- Go above and beyond what is expected. Leading means that you move out in front of the others so that they will strive to catch up with you.
- Share the credit for success with others who are a part of your organization in any way (board members and friends as well as staff).
- Shoulder failures alone. Ultimately, the measure of your strength will be how you reorganize after a crisis. Hold yourself accountable.
- Make sure you can take pride in your performance.
- Do not demand from your employees anything that you would not demand of yourself.

Best Practices for In-House Training

As mentioned at the beginning of this book, most staff developers would agree that the goal of staff development is to change individuals' knowledge, understanding, behaviors, skills, values, and beliefs. How does this relate to training workshops? In my experience, five components to training constitute "Best Practices," as outlined in the following section.

Five Components of Best Practices

In order for a program to meet the criterion of Best Practice, it must contain the following five components.

Theory Presentation

The first component of a good training workshop is the presentation of theory or the description of a new skill that would be useful to attain. Usually, this is an introduction, and can be accomplished in less than an hour. It is most often provided in a lecture style. This part of the program articulates a vision for change, the organization's goals, and what management expects from participants.

Modeling

This is a demonstration of the new skill or behavior. It might include a video demonstration in addition to the live demonstration. Modeling provides a supportive atmosphere for the implementation of the new skill.

Practice

The third component of training is the practice of a skill in a simulated setting. The audience participates, trying out the new skill. This can take as long as needed for participants to be comfortable with the changes.

Feedback

The trainer must give prompt feedback about the performance of the workshop participants. He or she must give feedback on all actions taken that are necessary to assess the changes.

Coaching

The fifth component is coaching. As the new idea or skill is being applied and tried, follow-up attention is given to the workshop participants. This reinforcement process can also be an intervention process if the participants seem not to have fully grasped the new changes or skills.

The rule of thumb seems to be that, the more the vision is communicated in the beginning, and the more the participants are encouraged to practice the new skills, and if the feedback and the interventions are provided, the more successful the program will be.

Successful Staff Development Programs

This section presents examples of some outstanding staff development programs that are in operation across the United States. They are presented here as models that can be adapted to fit the needs of your particular library. Their offerings vary from full online graduate programs to simpler tutorials. The programs are guided by the spectrum of activities that were defined by the American Library Association's (ALA) Second Congress on Professional Education (2000). These include, but are not limited to, continuing education, lifelong learning activities, training and skills development, intellectual nourishment, personal networking, exposure to new ideas, and professional refreshment and rejuvenation. The ALA committee recognized the various means of providing development, including workshops, conferences and other events, research and publication, professional reading, association activity, and networking. In some cases, libraries other than those for whom the sites were developed are invited to use them. Some of them are free; others require registration and a fee. I have simply listed these programs alphabetically; I have not ranked or rated them.

American Library Association

The ALA administers the H.W. Wilson Library Staff Development Grants. These grants provide the funds for libraries to send their staff to already established programs. Check out http://www.ala.org/awards grants/index.cfm for current opportunities. The following are some of the libraries that have recently received the grant and can be contacted for further information: DeKalb, Georgia; De Plaines, Illinois; University of Detroit; City University of New York; Fairfax County, Virginia; Topeka, Kansas; Southern Maine Regional Library System; University of Missouri; Rocky River, Ohio; Washoe County Library, Reno, Nevada; Prince George's County, Maryland; Orange County, Florida; Wakefield, Massachusetts; Broward County, Florida; Loyola University; Newport News, Virginia.

Amigos

This organization schedules web-based training in a live online classroom. A variety of courses on all topics are offered, on a central time zone schedule. This site offers in-depth courses as well as webinars that change monthly. Go to http://www.amigos.org for more information.

Austin Community College

This Texas college's program includes a blog for collecting and distributing all of the professional development opportunities offered by the staff development team at the library, including a Continuing Education Program, a Corporate Training Solutions Center, and a Business Assessment Center that is especially helpful to libraries. Visit http://www.austincc.edu for more details.

International Online Conference

This organization does just what its name implies—it provides webcasts and other online training opportunities. Go to http://www.international conference.org/ to see the many programs being offered.

Milwaukee Public Library

This large public library received a grant from Northwestern Mutual Foundation to offer free, two-hour, hands-on workshops. Held in the library and its various branches, these classes are open to anyone in the area who registers. These are especially helpful for doing research. Check out http://www.mpl.org/.

Ohio Library Council

One of the exciting programs offered by this organization is their orientation program, which is designed for new employees in the public library environment. This provides a basic library introduction, the mission, and an overview of services. You can check out these tutorials and a Webinar archive at http://www.olc.org/online-edu.asp.

Purdue University Libraries

This university library maintains a website for staff development and technology training. Information is updated monthly, so periodic checks of the site can be very beneficial. Go to http://www.lib.purdue.edu to learn more about their instructional services and CORE (Comprehensive Online Research Organization).

University of Illinois at Urbana-Champaign, Graduate School of Library and Information Science, Continuing Professional Development Program

This program is committed to providing the library and information professional community with a variety of continuing professional development opportunities. The university offers several activities in this area, with a wide range of opportunities available each semester. Visit http://www.lis.illinois.edu/academic/leep for more information.

In addition to the programs just mentioned, I would highly recommend the book *Staff Development Strategies That Work! Stories and Strategies from New Librarians*, edited by Georgie L. Donovan and Miguel A. Figueroa (New York: Neal-Schuman, 2009). In this book, new librarians share personal stories of their own successful professional development.

Mentoring as a Method of Staff Development

Mentoring can be achieved by pairing experienced employees with those who are new or less experienced. It is an often-overlooked method of providing staff development opportunities within our libraries. Before one begins to implement such a program, it is important to make sure the overall work environment is one that provides a supportive venue for staff development. In addition, the environment must be open and non-threatening. Employees need to be reassured that making mistakes is a natural part of the learning process. The mentor points out what "went wrong" and makes corrections for the next attempt. Employees need to be encouraged so that their confidence in their own abilities improves as they gain experience. Patience and repetition reinforce the learning process, and observing the skills of experienced employees serves to help newer employees. Pairing allows experienced employees to oversee the work of newer employees and showcase their own skills at the same time.

IN THIS CHAPTER:

✔ The Benefits of Mentoring Programs

✔ Costs Associated with Mentoring Programs

✔ Mentoring Relationships

✔ Developing a Mentoring Program

The Benefits of Mentoring Programs

For the Mentee

The best type of mentoring occurs when the relationship between new and experienced employees develops naturally. The chemistry between them makes them "click," and supportive relationships develop as a result. Modern trends in many organizations, however, include the institution of formal mentoring programs because they are so effective that the organizations cannot afford to wait for these relationships to happen by chance. One reason that this type of program is so effective is the importance of role-modeling: exhibiting desirable behavior is one of the best ways to encourage similar behavior in other employees.

The mentoring process provides employees a humanizing dimension that makes a difference in the long-term development of organizational teamwork. Employees learn who they can approach for assistance in

---

THE FOUR PHASES OF MENTORING

1. The initiation, when the mentor meets the new employee

2. The cultivation, during which the employee learns from the mentor

3. The separation, when the employee is now able to move away from the mentor and branch out on his or her own

4. The redefinition, when the employee and the mentor can redesign their relationship, support one another, continue their friendship, and ultimately, help someone else

---

difficult situations or when they need answers to questions. Introductions and making contacts are other aspects of the mentoring protocol. Through the mentoring process, mentees meet others in the library organization or in the community. Mentors can also help the newcomers become a part of the culture of the organization by explaining traditions and warning against difficult situations and politics. Because of the close working relationships that develop between mentors and those being mentored, mentors are often in the best position to evaluate the work of new employees and report their progress to supervisors and administrators.

Mentor relationships are really about professional success and personal growth. Mentors provide a safe haven for new employees because they provide a way for these individuals to test situations, to ask questions, and to make mistakes without embarrassment while ensuring they are learning. Mentors can help mentees formulate and guide work and career dreams.

In addition to being a role model who leads the way for employees, mentors are very important during the moments in an employee's career when decisions must be made. Mentors can help point out why a person would be good in a particular specialty, whether a try should be made for a promotion (Is he or she ready for it?), or even whether a career change should be considered. Mentors are usually in a position of power in the organization, and they are able to provide behind-the-scenes information ("Don't accept that position at X Library. Sally Jones is not returning in May, and you are being considered for her position"). They are able to introduce employees to members of the power structure and can both protect them and lobby for special assignments for them. Mentors demonstrate the values and the standards of the profession while promoting and enhancing a sense of competence and confidence in the employee. Very often, too, it is mentors who will cause employees to stretch their abilities, encouraging goals that the employee might have thought were beyond reach.

For the Mentor

Mentors benefit from the mentoring process as well. As with all relationships, the mentoring relationship is mutually beneficial if it is based on respect. Mentors begin to build power bases as individuals look up to them and as their good reputations spread. Mentors receive confirmation that their knowledge and experience are valuable. Mentoring gives mentors the opportunity to reflect on what they have learned and accomplished and to pass it on to others. This fits in with the classic definition of mentoring, which is the mutually beneficial relationship between two people that is based on the needs of both. It is a relationship that constantly changes and evolves. Ideally, mentors want their protégés to learn from them and then to surpass the mentors' capabilities. Mentorships present opportunities for people to shape themselves and to look within themselves for answers.

Mentors have the opportunity to receive a higher level of benefits from their peers because they have chosen to promote someone with potential. They gain respect because they have been developing talent, and the thriving of the new employee is a reflection of the mentors' good judgment. In many ways, being a mentor is a morale booster for experienced employees who may be looking for a new challenge. The mentoring experience offers the opportunity to stay in touch with new developments in the field by talking and working with people who have only recently completed their formal learning. It offers the chance to reappraise past performance and to appreciate how one's own career has developed, and even perhaps the chance to groom one's successor. When a person shares strength and wisdom, he or she becomes stronger, wiser, and more confident.

For the Organization

One should not overlook the benefits that the organization derives from encouraging and arranging mentoring opportunities. When mentoring succeeds, people have a sense of belonging, and their teamwork and their productivity increases. They are less likely to leave their positions because they feel a stronger commitment to the organization as well as a loyalty to the person who has guided them. This retention is important for continuity of service. Communications are also improved, and the mixing of styles strengthens the organization as newcomers are encouraged to apply different approaches and perspectives. Another natural development of mentoring is the evolution of smooth transitions and successions.

Costs Associated with Mentoring Programs

Mentoring programs take time and effort, and do involve costs. The cost can be determined by multiplying the amount of time that each staff member spends in the program in a given year by their hourly salary. Managers must also take into consideration staff time from the person who coordinates the program. Again, this time is dependent upon the size of the program, but it must be taken into account. However, mentoring is worth the cost. It has advantages for the staff members, of course, but having staff members who are committed to one another is a huge benefit for the library. As with everything, it is important to evaluate mentoring programs—and not just at the end of the program. Interim checks should be made so corrections can be made to the program if necessary. It is also important to go beyond the "feel good" data. Especially where a skill competency is desired, begin with a baseline, and evaluate competency, knowledge, and satisfaction. Only through evaluation will supervisors know if the library's mentoring program justifies the costs associated with it.

ADVANTAGES OF MENTORING PROGRAMS

- Mentoring programs will result in testimonials from those who have benefited from the positive influence of the program, thereby promoting the strengths of the organization.
- Role models and mentors are an important component of career development.
- Mentoring is almost a guarantee that someone cares about a participant's career.
- Mentors can use their personal contacts to help other employees.
- Retention is improved because loyalty to the organization develops.
- Mentoring programs create a knowledge-sharing environment, thereby benefiting the entire organization.

Mentoring Relationships

The Different Types

Different degrees and levels of mentoring relationships exist. The first level is between peers or colleagues. These relationships can provide a strong network of support and information among staff members, who can serve as sounding boards for one another. They can share experiences and inside information. They can compensate for one another's weaknesses as well as learn from one another. Peers can be very supportive mentoring partners, each filling the mentor and the protégé roles at various times in various situations. For example, an experienced staff member may not be current on all of the latest in technology, including Facebook, Twitter, and the like, while a newer, perhaps younger, employee may be an expert.

The next level of the mentoring relationship grows from a trainer relationship. Providing day-to-day, hands-on involvement helps employees improve their performance and prepare themselves for further advancement. In these relationships, the trainer must be honest and possess the ability to provide constructive criticism on behavior and performance. This type of relationship is goal oriented, focusing on developing new skills and strategies. The next step is when the trainer takes on further responsibility toward a particular employee and becomes his or her sponsor. In this relationship, the sponsor promotes the employee publicly, recognizing and drawing attention to skills and potential. The sponsor may make it possible for the employee to be put on special committees or task forces, receive promotions, or gain other recognition within the library or community.

Determining Who Should Mentor

Not all staff members would be comfortable being a mentor. This section provides a tool and some tips that are useful in helping staff members decide whether they would like to participate in a formal mentoring program, and in helping supervisors determine who among the current senior staff would work well with newer employees. It also provides tips for employees on how to be an effective mentor.

CHARACTERISTICS OF A GOOD MENTOR	
Accessible	Accurate
Competent	Nurturing
Successful	Supportive
Respectful	Protective
Good teacher/motivator	Aggressive
Inspires confidence	Assertive
Empathetic	Risk taking
Honest	Generous with credit and praise

Mentoring as a Method of Staff Development

One way staff members and supervisors can ascertain who might be an effective mentor is by using a mentor survey. For an example, see Figure 6.1.

Figure 6.1. Mentor Survey

Use this survey to evaluate yourself as a potential mentor. For each question, check all that apply.

1. Which of the following best describes you?
   - __ experienced employee
   - __ high level of responsibility
   - __ on a fast track
   - __ independent
   - __ looking for a new challenge
   - __ potential role model
   - __ confident in career

2. Do you enjoy helping less experienced people by:
   - __ teaching a specific skill?
   - __ helping them clarify goals?
   - __ introducing them to your organization?
   - __ providing specific information?
   - __ demonstrating how to accomplish their work?

3. Do you get a feeling of satisfaction from developing others by:
   - __ recognizing potential in employees?
   - __ providing support and encouragement?
   - __ teaching a specific set of skills?
   - __ encouraging them to try something new?
   - __ giving recognition to improve confidence and self-esteem?
   - __ discussing and promoting values?

4. Do you feel rewarded when helping others:
   - __ develop a team?
   - __ provide leadership for the team?
   - __ improve skills?
   - __ improve performance?

5. Do you enjoy:
   - __ counseling others?
   - __ giving advice?
   - __ providing encouragement?
   - __ proving recognition or praise?
   - __ recognizing performance that is up to standard/providing strategies for performance improvement?
   - __ helping people compensate for their limitations or those of the organization?

6. Are you able to:
   - __ push people when they need it?
   - __ evaluate performance that does not meet expectations and recommend changes?
   - __ provide development opportunities?
   - __ assign people to difficult tasks and help them succeed?
   - __ match individuals' skills and abilities to the organization's goals?

7. Are you able to help people with organizational structure by:
   - __ clarifying goals and objectives?
   - __ showing them how to contribute to organizational success?
   - __ promoting service standards?
   - __ explaining opportunities for growth and promotion?

8. You want to help or teach others because:
   - __ you want others to learn the profession.
   - __ you want to delegate responsibilities.
   - __ you want to increase your self-esteem as well as theirs.
   - __ you want to share your expertise.
   - __ you want to use the power of your position and reputation to help others.

If you have checked at least one-half of these, chances are you would be a good mentor to new employees.

HOW TO BE A GOOD MENTOR

- **Know when to give instructions and when to give orders.** Orders are appropriate when the employee knows how to complete a project that will meet your expectations, and you need to have a job done. Instructions are appropriate when you need to explain how to do something to someone who has not done the job before or when you are using a new method.

- **Tailor instruction to meet individual needs.** Staff members have different levels of understanding; you must keep these in mind. Ask them to let you know whether you are being too repetitive. Use a step-by-step process to explain tasks.

- **Speak the same language.** Avoid jargon unless you are sure the person knows this secret language of the profession.

- **Be specific.** Explain *what* you want, *when* it is due, *what* you expect completed, and *what* latitude the employee has in decision making.

- **Demonstrate.** Show the way so the employee can visualize what you want.

- **Explain your reasons.** If you explain why you are doing something, you help the employee understand how the project will affect the organization as a whole. This puts value on the task.

- **Stand and listen.** Employees are valuable contributors to our organization; pay attention to what is said and always read between the lines.

- **Provide feedback.** Let employees know you are satisfied with their work. If something is not right, give an explanation of why it is not and determine what caused the problem.

Role Model versus Mentor

Sometimes, the question is asked, "Is there a difference between a role model and a mentor?" The answer is definitely yes. A role model may be emulated from a distance and does not necessarily take on any of the mentoring responsibilities just mentioned. The role model may not even be aware that he or she is considered a role model. The wisdom one gains through experience must be passed on to others. In the final analysis, the most important part of being a leader may be that you have prepared someone else to take your place.

Developing a Mentoring Program

Mentoring programs are designed to support the professional development of staff members. Although a few recognized principles should be included in all programs, the mentoring program should be as unique as the library that it serves. In general, the library should develop a set of guidelines that remain consistent for all staff. These would include the length of time for the mentoring relationship. Typically, these relationships last for one year. The guidelines also should identify who is eligible for the program. This factor varies. In some libraries, only professional staff members are involved. In the best-case scenario, all staff members are eligible. Some libraries make the program available only to new employees. The library should also outline in the guidelines how often the mentor and the mentee are expected to meet, and if the meetings for the mentoring relationship are considered part of work time, which I strongly recommend. In addition, the library's guidelines should outline the procedure for becoming a part of the mentoring program and define what the library expects to get from the arrangement. Mentors can be a resource for professional development as well as an introduction to the library's particular system. They can provide introductions for the newcomer to get involved in local and national professional associations, and they can provide insider perspectives on working for the organization.

Matching Mentors with Mentees

In most cases, libraries use a formal process for matching mentors with mentees. This is most often accomplished by the individuals completing a questionnaire that determines what it is they expect to gain from the relationship and what their specific areas of interest/accomplishments are. This formal process is best when the program goals are clearly explained and are linked to the library's mission. It also clearly identifies the roles for all participants, lists the competencies on which the program will focus, and specifies the time commitment expected.

Some organizations have one-on-one mentoring programs. These are especially effective when both the library and the staff member want to achieve a specific goal. For example, the local history librarian may take a newcomer as a mentee to teach him or her what is in the collection and/or introduce the newcomer to those who are knowledgeable in the community (e.g., a local history buff, or the local historical society). This benefits mentors, as they are able to share their expertise and may get some much-needed person power from the people they train, and it benefits mentees, who are developing a specialty. In addition, it is of great value to the library to have someone prepared to take over the reins if the original staff member chooses to retire or resign.

Another option is to have a group mentoring program. In this type of program, one or two mentors work with a group of people who have some need in common. It may be a group of new hires who need an orientation to the system, or perhaps it is a group of newly promoted supervisors who need to learn the intricacies of management.

Organizations also have another option, known as a reverse mentoring program. In this type of program, a senior employee is paired with a new employee who may have just finished their library degree. This is a win-win situation, as the new employee learns about the particular organization from someone who has been in the system for a while, and the senior employee learns what the new trends are from the newcomer.

Examples of Successful Mentoring Programs

One example of a well-established mentoring program is the SCOPA Mentoring Program at the Yale University Library (http://www.library .yale.edu/scopa/ mentoring.html). This program is designed to support the professional development of the Yale librarians. It orients newcomers to the system and opens communication between those at different levels and in different departments of the system. It is open to anyone in the Yale system who is interested in making connections with colleagues.

The University of Georgia Libraries participates in Project Promote (http://www.uga.edu). This resource is intended to offer active support for career development. The portal website is designed to address the hesitancy of articulating questions and concerns from newcomers to those more established. The site acts as a mentoring community; members can post a question anonymously, and it will be answered by an identified senior faculty member. Other resources are also included.

Mentoring eventually becomes a responsibility for all in the profession when we begin to think of work as more than a job—when we realize that we will be doing this work for the rest of our lives. Passing on our career goals to others who are new to the profession is a way to reinforce and extend those goals. If conducted correctly and effectively, the mentoring process will be extremely beneficial to mentor, mentee, and the organization.

Development Opportunities Outside of Your Library

One of the simplest ways to promote staff development is to encourage participation in professional associations, and, if at all possible, pay the membership fees for these. While these types of organizations certainly offer training opportunities, simply conferring with a network of people within the same profession is a development tool in itself.

Another, sometimes overlooked, opportunity is transferring skills to other appropriate situations. A library is, by definition, learning centered. Staff members use their skills to perform their jobs; they can also use these skills to assist other community agencies. For instance, if a library staff member is especially good at developing websites, perhaps this person can assist another agency with theirs. This could provide an opportunity to barter training; perhaps that agency's staff member has expertise in an area where the library needs help. At the very least, this is one of the ways in which the library can build goodwill in the community.

These are just a few examples of how the library can find ways to offer development at a low cost. Detailed in the following paragraphs are several more no-cost or low-cost suggestions for staff development.

Relationships with Colleagues

It is important that your library develop relationships with the libraries in neighboring towns. Their staffs, of course, will have many of the same professional challenges that your staff has. They may also share some other, non-professional issues (for example, public transportation may be sorely lacking in the area). If you share the same challenges, then it is more than likely that you can economize on solutions by sharing those, as well. What can you do together to improve library services? Can the two staffs be trained on some strategies together? One of the solutions may be that you both share the cost of a trainer, and bring the staffs together at one location for the session. Another scenario would be to send some employees to a training session that the other library is hosting; you reciprocate by inviting some of their staff to your next training.

IN THIS CHAPTER:

✔ Relationships with Colleagues

✔ State and Regional Library Services

✔ Professional Associations

✔ Relationships with Similar Agencies

✔ Chambers of Commerce

✔ Partnerships with Local Companies

✔ Community Colleges and Universities

✔ E-learning

✔ Other Forms of Continuing Education

WHY SHOULD LIBRARIES TRY TO COLLABORATE?

- Cooperation is important.
- Organizations can pool their common interests, assets, and professional skills.
- This is an economical way to enhance opportunities.
- The library can contain costs while maximizing program benefits.

Another option is for some staff members from one library "covering the desk" at another library so staff members can attend an out-of-library workshop. These strategies work especially well for libraries that are within an easy, relatively short, driving distance to each other.

Another way to learn is by taking field trips to other libraries. If a library director is aware that another library is a shining example of a new and innovative service, taking staff members there to see it in action is a wonderful training opportunity. Staff members can clearly visualize what is happening, and they can make the adaptations and adjustments that may be needed to make the program work in your library.

State and Regional Library Services

Although it differs from state to state, most of the state library organizations offer a variety of opportunities for the libraries within their areas. Since these are often subsidized by tax dollars, it is usually very affordable to participate in them. Membership in professional organizations may make these even more affordable by providing a membership discount. Some states have regional offices in which various meetings, classes, continuing-education opportunities, and trainings are held, making access to them easy and affordable. Because part of the mission of these groups is library development, the offerings are relevant and intended to assist libraries in performance standards. The Resource Directory at the end of this book includes a listing of these agencies.

Professional Associations

Professional associations often offer training programs that are specific to the profession and usually at a cost that is very affordable. In addition, holding a membership in the organization may save even more money. The library director should encourage staff members to take advantage of these, and should provide the scheduling flexibility that will allow them to attend. Many times these programs are focused on a particular specialty (children's librarians, reference librarians); this makes it easier on the library staff to keep the library open while staff is away, because only certain staff members need to attend. In addition to the new skills that are acquired, those attending are able to network with colleagues from across a region or state. Sharing similar challenges and successes is another informal way staff development happens at these events.

Relationships with Similar Agencies

Schools and museums are two types of organizations that have issues similar to libraries. In fact, many school districts require in-service trainings on a regular basis. What is your relationship with your school district? Their in-service trainings may be addressing issues that apply to the general population of the town, or issues that are relevant to all types of employees (for example, workplace violence or diversity training). They certainly offer grade-specific training that may be appropriate for some staff members. It is beneficial to build a relationship with the administrators, and simply ask whether there is room for your staff in any of their sessions. Again, this is another opportunity to reciprocate training: The teachers need to know about library services. Perhaps you have an expert on local history on staff, or someone who is on the cutting edge of a new technology. Can your library provide a workshop for the school system on a particular topic? In my experience, this turns into a barter relationship, and no money is involved. This is a method that I have found to be a win-win for all concerned.

Chambers of Commerce

The local Chamber of Commerce is based on a national model, the purpose of which is to support and develop business within a given area. While the library is not a "business" per se, it is an important component of the community, and falls under the purview of the mission of the Chamber of Commerce. A library should strongly consider membership in their local Chamber. First of all, the Chamber of Commerce directly offers training courses to its members. Leadership development seminars, marketing, and public relations are some of the types of workshops provided. In addition, membership in the Chamber provides the library administrator with the opportunity to network and make connections with local businesses. This may lead to further training opportunities. It may also help the library make contacts for other reasons (such as speakers, donations, or capital campaigns). Serving on a committee of the Chamber also gives the library a presence in the community. Community members see the librarian's skills, and this helps develop relationships that often prove fruitful. The fees the Chamber charges for its services are minimal, especially if the library holds a membership.

Partnerships with Local Companies

Many local companies offer a variety of training opportunities for their employees. In an effort to help the community, they may agree to assist the library by admitting some library staff members into some of their workshops, if those workshops are not based on trade secrets. While this type of program is not library specific, the offerings can cover a range of topics that are universal in theme, such as sensitivity training, team building, first aid/CPR, and conflict resolution. Again, attending these types of events can also provide good public relations opportunities as the staff mingles with the companies' employees.

Community Colleges and Universities

While these institutions offer degree programs, many of them also offer certificate and continuing education courses that can be helpful for staff. Many times these are offered for far less than regular tuition charges. Usually labeled as noncredit, they often are held during intersessions. If chosen carefully, these courses can greatly benefit the library staff.

E-learning

A plethora of opportunities are now available on the Internet. Not all of them are free, but many do offer opportunities that were just not possible before. The benefits of e-learning are that people can take classes at a time that is convenient for them, and travel time is eliminated. Another advantage is that the student is able to try out the materials in private, without the pressure of performing in a group. This type of learning is especially useful when only one or two staff members want or require education on a particular subject, and it is not cost-effective to pay for a live event. State universities, city colleges, and private companies all offer e-learning because it makes their programs much more accessible to more people.

Web conferences and "webinars" are another growing area of opportunity for continuing education. Because of their nature, they are able to reach many more people than a traditional conference or seminar. They also make it possible for the sponsoring organization to offer the very best resource person(s) for the training. They provide the advantage of no travel for the participants. Depending upon the sponsoring organization, these can be free, very inexpensive, or expensive. Some of these are "mini," meaning that they are intended to present one concept or skill, while others are much more comprehensive and may be more general in nature, providing an overview, rather than a focused training. Some of these are interactive. With the constant upgrades in technology, the popularity of this method of providing continuing education continues to grow.

Other Forms of Continuing Education

Several types of opportunities provide a means for this type of continued learning for individuals. One must consider the skills that one is interested in obtaining when deciding to choose this delivery method. Some of these may require a certificate upon completion: first aid and CPR training are two such examples. Other courses may not be directly related to library work, but are still important to the person taking them. For instance, a staff member may want to develop his or her photography skills to record events at the library. A class offered by the local Adult Education Department may be sufficient for this purpose.

E-LEARNING WEBSITES FOR LIBRARIANS

Some outstanding websites that offer online courses for libraries are listed here.

- California State University, http://www.ce.csueastbay.edu/courses/distance-learning.shtml
- Ohio State University, http://www.ohiostateonline.com
- Purdue University Library, http://www.distance.purdue.edu/
- The University of Phoenix, http://www.phoenix.edu
- The University of Wisconsin Online, http://www.wisconline.com

Other materials are included in Chapter 12, "Resource Directory."

Use of this type of program is best when it is the focus of one or two individuals, not the entire staff.

Library management should be supportive of ongoing learning. At times, this might require providing flexible work schedules so employees can attend these classes. Although this may take some juggling of schedules, most often a library can accommodate employees. The payoff will be worth this small inconvenience.

Professional development of staff members promotes good library service. The examples in this chapter show that there are many ways to proceed. The library must consider these and other factors that may be particular to their library to find the most efficient, cost-effective method of accommodating staff development. In addition to a staff that provides great service, another benefit is the development of employee loyalty, and with that retention of solidly trained staff for the organization.

Model Training Programs

The aim of this book is to provide assistance to library managers. It is intended to help develop strategies to provide necessary, day-to-day training to address needs that arise in their organizations. The models that follow are meant to be resources. Training is crucial if our libraries' employees are going to achieve a uniform standard of performance. We want our service to be the same every hour we are open, not just when a particular employee is "on desk." No two librarians are the same, just as no two people are the same, so it is strongly recommended that these materials be used as models. For your program to reach maximum effectiveness, you will want to adapt and change portions of the models to make them more suitable for your needs. In addition, be sure to coordinate your program so that it will focus on those areas which are most critical for your library.

The following sections present sample training models that can be adapted for any type of library. All training sessions must have a period of summary or conclusion, which will tie up loose ends, allow participants to ask questions, and set the direction for the implementation of the new skill.

Effective Communication

This first program is designed to improve both internal communication within the library and the oral and written communication that the library uses with patrons and the community. The program provides ways to evaluate the status of communication that is presently in your library. It is most effective when it is completed by both the administration and as many staff members as possible. One of the interesting findings may be that the staff members and the director perceive the communication differently. This indicates a communication gap. The results of this audit will help the trainer develop the curriculum he or she will use for the training. Training of this type is best done when the trainer has at least two hours to spend with the staff. It can be even more effective if the training can be carried out over two two-hour sessions. The handouts

REASONS FOR GOOD COMMUNICATION

- To transmit information regarding the achievements and plans of the organization
- To disseminate creative ideas and practices that work
- To communicate cares, standards, concerns, and needs from bottom to top and top to bottom
- To transmit standards, mores, and organizational culture

that are provided as examples can be given to the participants at the conclusion of the first session, with the intent that they be completed and brought with them to start the second session. The method of training that will be used for this topic (or any topics) will vary by the trainer. In communication training, however, taped audio and video examples to illustrate both good and poor communication situations is most helpful. Role-playing is especially useful as well. Figures 8.1 through 8.4 (see pp. 62–64) provide valuable information on communication in the workplace.

Effective Communication Training Outline

Training objective: To improve the basic process of communication to help people help one another
Training methods to be used: Discussion, role-playing, brainstorming
Training aids: Blackboard, flip charts, PowerPoint, handouts

I. Why Is Effective Communication So Necessary?
  A. People need to understand one another.
    1. They need to transfer information and get a point across.
    2. They need to create working relationships; they work with a better attitude.
  B. An atmosphere of caring and concern is created by communication.
    1. It helps us realize that because others care, we are willing to share.
    2. Openness eliminates misunderstanding.

Figure 8.1. Effective Communication Training: The Audit

Before holding the training, the manager should evaluate the way the organization is communicating internally and externally. This will help provide some relevant examples for the trainer. The audit may also result in disclosing the reason for the perceived need for further improving communication.

Library Communication Audit

Always	Often	Never	
___	___	___	1. Are regular newsletters provided for all employees?
___	___	___	2. Are all staff members given advanced notice of library-related functions?
___	___	___	3. Are internal committees used for projects?
___	___	___	4. Are the media informed of staff accomplishments?
___	___	___	5. Is the library represented at community meetings?
___	___	___	6. Are staff members involved in planning?
___	___	___	7. Does the staff know the library board and vice versa?
___	___	___	8. Do supervisors relate what is happening at meetings?
___	___	___	9. Are regular staff meetings held?
___	___	___	10. Is time made for informal discussions between staff and the administration?

Figure 8.2. Effective Communication Training Handout 1: Overview

I. The Tools of Communication
- Being able to listen to another person
- Being able to write a letter of thanks
- Being able to write a note just to say hello
- Being able to write a letter of confirmation or a follow-up to what you have agreed to verbally
- Being able to write instructions
- Being able to use the telephone and e-mail wisely
- Being able to leave complete messages so the receiver understands even if he or she has not talked with you in person

II. How the World Today Communicates
- Person-to-person meetings each day
- Telephones
- Texting
- Facebook
- Twitter
- Fax machines
- Television
- Radio
- Movies and video documentaries
- Program performances
- Newspapers
- Magazines and other print resources
- CDs and audiotapes

III. How You Can Become a Good Communicator
- Be a person who cares for others and conveys it.
- Show that you have a positive attitude and you are excited about life.
- Write little notes and memos— they matter.
- Write letters for all different reasons.
- Use the telephone efficiently.
- Train yourself to sit down more often and listen to what another person is telling you.
- Keep working at it. Some things will become routine, but continual communication is important.

Figure 8.3. Effective Communication Training Handout 2: Self-Evaluation

Use the following evaluation to assess your communication skills.

Yes	No	Needs Improvement	
_____	_____	_____	I pay attention when introduced to others and remember their names.
_____	_____	_____	I smile when around other people.
_____	_____	_____	I resist opportunities to beat my own drum.
_____	_____	_____	I look for opportunities to compliment others.
_____	_____	_____	I am interested in others and what they have to say.
_____	_____	_____	I notice little things like birthdays and remember them.
_____	_____	_____	I avoid arguments at all costs.
_____	_____	_____	If I must criticize, I begin with a positive statement.
_____	_____	_____	I restate points of agreement whenever there may be a conflict.
_____	_____	_____	I give others the opportunity to bow out gracefully and save face.
_____	_____	_____	I don't say things like "I told you so."
_____	_____	_____	I ask questions designed to produce the answers I need.
_____	_____	_____	I ask questions and make requests rather than giving orders.
_____	_____	_____	I organize thoughts before I speak.
_____	_____	_____	I realize that communication is most accurate when kept simple.
_____	_____	_____	I am aware of the gestures and phrases I use.
_____	_____	_____	I realize people do things for their own reasons, not mine.
_____	_____	_____	I always try to act naturally, admit my mistakes, and show my sincerity through my actions.

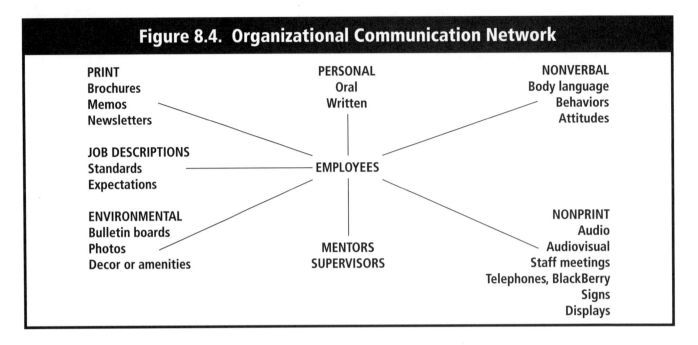

Figure 8.4. Organizational Communication Network

PRINT
Brochures
Memos
Newsletters

JOB DESCRIPTIONS
Standards
Expectations

ENVIRONMENTAL
Bulletin boards
Photos
Decor or amenities

PERSONAL
Oral
Written

EMPLOYEES

MENTORS
SUPERVISORS

NONVERBAL
Body language
Behaviors
Attitudes

NONPRINT
Audio
Audiovisual
Staff meetings
Telephones, BlackBerry
Signs
Displays

II. What Is Communication All About?

A. People understanding one another
   1. Communication is designed to produce response.
   2. Feedback is response, and it indicates how well a message was received.

B. Communication is about relationships; it is a two-way process.
   1. There is a sender and a receiver. Listening is one-half of the process.
   2. Every person communicates according to his or her ability to understand.

C. Communication is a people process.
   1. Thought and feeling will indicate if you are on common ground.
   2. Maturity will lead you to withhold judgment until you have enough facts and will cause you to listen respectfully even when you are not in agreement.

III. What Are the Barriers That Affect the Communication Process?

A. Sender barriers
   1. Attitude about the message or the receivers
   2. Poor communication skill—including unclear vocabulary and an inappropriate time, place, or method of delivering the message
   3. Prejudices
   4. Style

B. Receiver barriers
   1. Attitude about the message or the sender, including distrust and fear
   2. Message is too complicated

3. The person is preoccupied and not really listening or understanding

C. Communication breakdown happens if . . .
  1. The sender does not check for feedback regarding the understanding of the message.
  2. The receiver indicates understanding has taken place when it really hasn't.

IV. Tips for Being a Good Communicator

A. Make the receiver feel as if he or she is the only person in the world.
  1. Be sensitive and aware.
  2. Take an interest in others.
  3. Smile.

B. Know what you need to say.
  1. Be specific and direct.
  2. Keep message clear in terms that will be understood.
  3. Be positive.

C. The key to the receiver being interested is the need for information; interest in sender.
  1. Accept the fact that people do things for their own reasons.
  2. Adjust the message to meet the circumstances.

D. Be yourself.
  1. Be sincere.
  2. Don't pretend to know something you do not or to be something you are not.

V. Conclusion

A. Communication is a two-way process.
B. The value of the experience of communication is enhanced by applying these principles.

Orientation

The following program is an example of one that is useful to offer to new employees. It can be offered either in a group or on a one-to-one basis, depending upon institutional needs. Orientation programs serve both the employees and the organization. They provide a means for the introduction of newcomers to the staff and policies of their new employer, and a way to make newcomers feel comfortable in their new environment; and they provide the library with a way to explain all the institutional "housekeeping" that is always necessary. If the employer has an employee handbook or other written manual, this would be an appropriate time for distribution. The library can use the handout in Figure 8.5 (see p. 66) for this if it does not have a manual of its own.

Depending upon the size of the organization, I would recommend a four- to eight-hour orientation program. Spending a little bit more time at the outset will save time later. It would also be appropriate to have

Figure 8.5. Orientation Training Handout

Welcome!

Everyone has new job jitters. It is normal to wonder whether you'll fit in, whether you will like the job, or whether you will be able to perform it well. Accept the fact that it will be confusing at first and do not be too hard on yourself! Here are some things to do to help reduce the confusion of your new workplace.

1. Take some time to explore the library and observe the staff in action. Familiarity with the facility will help you reduce your fear of the unknown, and it will help you prepare for what you should expect.

2. Learn the basics as quickly as you can. Use introductions as a chance to gather useful information about your new coworkers. You'll be able to find out what people do, and you will begin to understand how your work will relate to them.

3. When in doubt, ask for advice or direction. Most people are especially kind to new employees because they remember what it was like for them.

4. Avoid developing a reputation as a critic. If you think of ways to improve current procedures, wait for the appropriate time to share them. People appreciate fresh points of view, but do not necessarily want to be told that the way they have been doing things is wrong.

5. Service to patrons is your first priority. You are joining a staff whose prime objective is to provide the very best possible library service. Keep the patron in mind at all times, and you will do just fine.

the employee rotate through the various departments of the system to become familiar with the entire operation. Time for this will vary, but a minimum of a few days is really necessary for the person to absorb the knowledge that is needed.

Orientation Training Outline

Training objective: To provide information to employees to assist them in the performance of their specific job

Program purpose: To communicate the organizational philosophy, mission, and goals and to provide clear expectations to new employees

Training aids: Handouts, organizational videos/slide shows

Evaluation: Adaptation of new employees to the organization: one-to-one sessions between employees and supervisors at the end of the probationary period

I. Philosophy Statement
   A. History and achievements of the library
      1. Important achievements
      2. Current status
      3. Future directions, goals, and objectives
   B. Mission statement
      1. Provides employees with a broad perspective on the organization
      2. Sets the stage for the employees' participation in helping the library achieve its goals
      3. Includes factors (programs, etc.) that make your library unique

C. Sample philosophy inclusions
1. Teamwork: Good library service results when it's everyone's job.
2. Treat employees like patrons—with respect and courtesy.
3. Quality: Do the job right.
4. Value: Make people feel that they are getting their money's worth.

II. Library Standards, Procedures, and Policies

A. Standards
1. Clearly written statements of expectations
2. Performance standards as they relate to job descriptions

B. Procedures and policies
1. Overview of the operations
2. Operations manual
3. Employee's role within the division or department

III. Employment Logistics

A. Tour of the facility
1. Floor plan, evacuation plan overview, lounge facilities
2. Staff introductions

B. Employee benefits
1. Details of the employee's contract
2. Overview of general benefits and pay periods

C. Chain of command

IV. Library Opportunities

A. Opportunities for development
1. Internal seminars, courses
2. Participation in workshops, seminars, and conferences
3. Encouragement of formal education and explanation of reimbursement policies

B. Opportunities for advancement
1. Probationary period
2. Promotion possibilities

V. On-Site Training

A. Position training
1. Responsibilities defined
2. Supervised jobs

B. Library training
1. Cross-training with other departments
2. Relationships between departments

VI. Evaluation

A. Performance evaluations
1. Each employee is different and will respond to the training based on his or her own motivation, intelligence, personality, and willingness to work.

2. Training should send a message to the employee about the quality, caring, and professionalism of the organization.

B. Conclusion

1. The training should result in the employee's feeling more comfortable with the job.
2. Supervisors have the opportunity to assess the employee's abilities and skills and determine if the employee is appropriately matched to the position.
3. Administration's most important decision is to select people and determine their performance capabilities. Failure to train them properly can have devastating consequences: poor performances, low productivity, the need for increased supervision, heightened employee turnover, discipline and motivation problems in the workplace.

Teamwork

Every organization is more successful when the people within it are able to work together as a team. The teamwork training program can be used as a follow-up to the orientation training, or it can be used as a refresher course for employees who have been with the organization for a while. It is especially beneficial to do the training with every department head or supervisor, and then have each one use these newly learned skills to develop a team. It is training that can be implemented over a period of time, rather than in one two-hour training slot. A word of advice: Teamwork training is not something that can be done once and then forgotten. As with any team, the coaching process must be ongoing. To be effective, the library director must recognize this need for continual coordination and direction. Many libraries have staff report to work an hour before the library opens to patrons. Usually this is to have time to perform background jobs while no patrons are in the building. However, this is also a good time to schedule ongoing training; the frequency will depend on staff size and how much material you want the trainer to cover. Figures 8.6 and 8.7 (see pp. 69–70) present handouts for use during teamwork training.

Teamwork Training Outline

Training objective: To develop effective teams in order to reach objectives

Training purpose: An organization's success is determined by the attitudes, behavior, and performance of all employees. Working together will provide a more efficient way of accomplishing goals.

Training methods: Small group sessions with brainstorming; handouts; mentoring

Training aids: Motivational posters and tapes

Evaluation: Performance of the library is measured against job requirement fulfillments and the perceptions of performance standards.

Figure 8.6. Teamwork Training Handout 1: Teamwork Planning Wheel

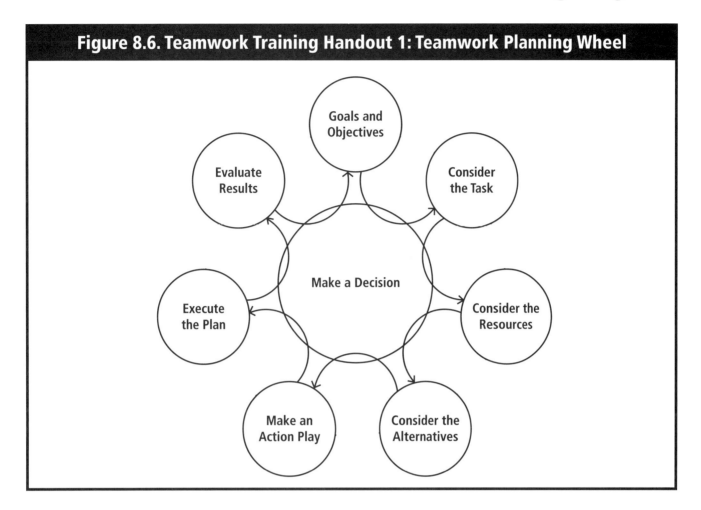

I. How to Build the Team

  A. Identify the organization's goals.
    1. What is the job?
    2. What are you trying to do?

  B. All must have a clear understanding of their tasks and responsibilities.
    1. What will help get the job done?
    2. What will hamper us in getting the job done?

II. How to Identify the Strengths of the Employees

  A. Inventory each person's strengths.
    1. Match strengths with activities.
    2. Force each individual to look beyond the scope of his or her own efforts and consider how his or her strengths fit into the scope of the organization's goals.

  B. Learn from one another.
    1. Break down status differentials.
    2. Recognize that status is based on experience, but that every person has worthwhile contributions to make and needs the opportunity to reach his or her potential.

Figure 8.7. Teamwork Training Handout 2: Thinking about Teamwork

Teamwork results when interrelated elements bring a group of individuals into cohesive units that function together and work to achieve the organization's goals. The following are some requirements for teamwork.

- You must learn how to work together.
- You must learn to play on one another's strengths because it makes the team stronger.
- You must learn to be part of the solution when someone makes a mistake.

Teams should establish:

- their work standards;
- the sequence of their work;
- the production process;
- the tools that will be used;
- their schedules in cooperation with the overall needs of the organization.

Don't duplicate efforts. Teams increase cooperation, spur new ideas, and inspire product quality.

III. Adopt Participatory Management as a Guide

    A. Everyone has the duty and responsibility to influence decision making.

        1. People need to understand the diversity of individual employees' gifts.

        2. People must trust and respect one another.

    B. Participatory management provides the environment that allows momentum to develop.

        1. An aggressive, professionally driven organization will result.

        2. Team members will be able to make a meaningful difference in the organization.

        3. Lead by example so your style is copied and passed on to other people.

        4. Appreciate constructive discontent (i.e., employees' always finding ways to improve their work).

IV. The Team Needs to Help Develop the Vision

    A. Vision is about what the organization could and should be.

        1. All who have a stake in the organization participate in creating the vision.

        2. Leadership includes figuring out the right things to do to approach the vision.

    B. Strategies must be rooted in understanding.

        1. Fiscal considerations

        2. Personnel resources

V. Building a Strong Implementation Network

    A. Leadership involves risk-taking.

        1. Risk-taking involves unknown consequences.

        2. Risk-taking can be motivating and thus influence team building.

B. Strategies for teamwork success
  1. Supportive relationships with key sources and resources
  2. Cooperative environment
  3. Motivation to make visions become reality

VI. Conclusion
  A. Leaders leave behind them assets and a legacy so that someone else can take over.
  B. Leaders are obligated to create a team of followers whose lives and work are intertwined so that they can reach a goal.

Time Management

I think most people would agree that we all could use more time. Everyone has twenty-four-hour days, yet some people are able to get so much more done than others. The key is not that they have more time, but rather that they know how to use their time much more efficiently. The following training program will provide both tips and strategies so that your staff will learn how to use its time more efficiently. It is followed by a handout (see Figure 8.8, p. 72) that should help the individual focus on the organization of his or her duties to conserve time. This handout can also aid troubleshooting because it points out time-wasters and offers some solutions for change.

Time Management Training Outline

Training objective: To assist staff members in developing organization skills for their time

Training purpose: With the current trend of staff reductions, it has become even more critical to work effectively and efficiently.

Training methods: Small group sessions; handouts; hands-on practice on implementing newfound skills

Training aids: Posters, calendars, any organizing units (traditional, or new technologies)

Evaluation: More tasks are accomplished within the workday.

I. Time Management Is Life Management
  A. Employees need to develop a sense of urgency about tasks.
    1. Priorities must be set for tasks.
    2. Tasks must be actions that will help organizations reach goals.
  B. Priorities will be achieved if urgency is associated with tasks.
    1. Staff must learn how to complete tasks.
    2. Do the most important things first.

II. Organizing Tasks Reduces Stress
  A. Stress occurs when the individual believes the demands of a situation are more than he or she can handle.
    1. An internal support system can help overcome this.
    2. Rotation of workload and responsibilities can help.

Figure 8.8. Time Management Training Handout: Self-Evaluation

Evaluate your day to see if you are wasting time. Then develop a plan to help you be more organized and to use your time more wisely.

Schedule

1. How many deadlines do I normally have every day?
2. Are these deadlines self-imposed?
3. Could any of these tasks be postponed? Done another way? Not done at all?
4. How many of these tasks are handled by me only? Can they be done by someone else?
5. What happens if I do not complete these tasks or meet the deadlines?
6. How do I feel at the end of the day? Exhausted? Tired? Worn out? Satisfied? Frustrated?

Meetings

1. Is this meeting necessary? How else might I accomplish this task?
2. Do participants come well-prepared and well-organized? If not, what can I do to change this?
3. Do meetings start and finish on time?
4. Is there an agenda?
5. Is the meeting's purpose clearly understood?
6. Does everyone leave the meeting with action plans that are well-defined and agreed upon?

     B. Change your perception of stress.
       1. Keep realistic goals.
       2. List positive achievements.
       3. Self-esteem is the foundation of competence.

III. Emphasize Effectiveness
     A. Organizations need to evaluate their processes.
       1. Ninety percent of wasted time can be eliminated with a little common sense.
       2. Use information to develop time-saving advantages.
     B. Projects can be changed to use time more efficiently.
       1. Use downtime to accomplish large projects all at once.
       2. Develop plans in advance to be ready for this.

IV. Personal Development Is a Springboard to Efficiency
     A. Continuing to learn puts us at an advantage.
       1. Develop skills.
       2. Develop personalities.
     B. Balance your life.
       1. Learn to take time for yourself.
       2. Learn to be your own best asset.

V. Conclusion
     A. Use aids that will work for you.
       1. Use technology as a helpful resource.
       2. Organize work for efficiency.

B. Teamwork helps time management.
   1. Working together increases efficiency.
   2. Everyone is working for the same goals.
   3. No one has more time than another; success is proportionate to how well time is utilized and managed.

TIME MANAGEMENT HINTS

- Respect time and do not waste it. Wasted time decreases the time available for profitable use.
- Analyze and budget your time. Examine how you spend your time and determine how much you actually need to accomplish tasks.
- Do the job(s) you do not like to do first. It is a real motivator to accomplish tasks that you find difficult, boring, etc.
- Make a "to do" list and prioritize everything you must do. Finish each item before you go on to the next. Cross out items when done; it will make you feel you have accomplished something.
- Make appointments for specific times.
- Use the telephone properly. Prepare for each call. List points you want to cover. Keep calls brief and to the point.
- If you reach a voice mail, or need to leave a message, leave an action message so the person you are calling will know what you need done. This is the same for e-mail. This is much more efficient than simply asking the person to get back to you.
- Use a calendar. A pocket calendar, a portable computer calendar, or programs on your PC should be updated daily and reviewed weekly. Be sure to include all appointments, deadlines, and commitments.
- Record thoughts and ideas on index cards, in a small notebook, or on tape. Add these to your files as you update them.
- Devote 80 percent of your time to the top 20 percent of your priorities.
- List your major projects for the year. Rearrange them in order of priority.
- Identify your major projects for the month, put them in priority order, and then develop your work schedule for the week.
- Confirm appointments to avoid wasting transit time.
- Control your open-door policy. Although a good manager is accessible, you need uninterrupted time to yourself to concentrate.
- Use new technologies to help you work smarter, not harder.
- Create some quiet time for yourself. You need some to recharge.
- Remember: People measure you by your accomplishments, not by the number of hours that you have worked. Get things done, but efficiently.

Customer Service

Customer service, or service to our user communities, is without a doubt one of the major portions of a library staff's job. It is a learned skill that at times can be frustrating, but it is also the area in which most of us feel most rewarded. It is a vital link between our organization and the people we serve. Each person in the organization is a link in a service chain that searches out, acquires, processes, catalogs, and provides materials, information, and service to our patrons. Only as a complete, interactive team can we serve our users' needs fully and efficiently. Customer expectations are higher than they ever were before, so in libraries we are faced with changing the way all of the employees think about themselves and their patrons.

Institution of a customer service program in the library needs to be done in phases. During the first phase, the library administrator must make an audit of the current levels of service in the library. The resulting awareness must include a realization that some things must change. Next, a commitment to the process must be made by the governing body of the library as well as by the administration. The staff development component is the next phase, in which actual training sessions are held with the staff. Part of the training will be developing the commitment of the staff to the process. Putting the plan into action follows. An evaluation process is an absolute must. Components of it must be from the insiders, but we must also make some tools available to gather input from our customer base. Our quality will be defined by the users, since it is our ability to meet their needs and then go on to exceed their expectations that is the essence of customer service. Figure 8.9 (see p. 75) provides a handout for use in customer service training.

Customer Service Training Outline

   I. Introduction
      A. Description of customer service
      B. Library's customer service philosophy

  II. Customer Service Audit Process
      A. Internal evaluation of what is in place
      B. Community service for patrons

 III. Ten Steps to Service Success
      A. Recognize the points of encounter (where employees have contact with the users).
         1. This is where you win or lose users.
         2. Observe and analyze service interactions, frequently putting yourself into the role of the user.
      B. Identify problem areas of service.
         1. Service desks as outlets of service
         2. Logistical arrangement of resources
         3. Identify opportunities that stand out and points that need correction.
      C. Develop plan of action for implementing changes to improve service.
         1. Ideas become solutions to the deficiencies.
         2. New approaches are added to improve service.
      D. Prioritize service execution.
         1. List community needs in order of priority.
         2. Establish service goals to meet these priorities.

Figure 8.9. Customer Service Training Handout 1: Self-Assessment

Please check the appropriate response.

Frequently	Sometimes	Never	
_____	_____	_____	1. Project an open, friendly attitude to all.
_____	_____	_____	2. Respond to complaints in a courteous and sympathetic manner.
_____	_____	_____	3. Use effective and attentive listening skills.
_____	_____	_____	4. Ask a telephone caller permission to be put on hold.
_____	_____	_____	4a. Thank the caller when I return.
_____	_____	_____	5. Follow the transaction until the patron is satisfied.
_____	_____	_____	6. Apologize even when it is not my fault.
_____	_____	_____	7. Provide timely responses to requests.
_____	_____	_____	8. Give equal consideration to telephone and in-person user.
_____	_____	_____	9. Provide assistance without being asked.
_____	_____	_____	10. Respond positively—what I can do, not what I cannot do.
_____	_____	_____	11. Speak clearly at all times.
_____	_____	_____	12. Show I am courteous.
_____	_____	_____	13. Maintain a nonjudgmental attitude toward customers' questions.
_____	_____	_____	14. Communicate on the level of the customer with no jargon.
_____	_____	_____	15. Identify my branch/department, give my name, and offer to help when answering the phone.
_____	_____	_____	16. Acknowledge others for providing good customer service.

E. Reallocate resources to meet new service goals.
  1. Financial
  2. Personnel
  3. Equipment, collection
F. Recruit other personnel.
  1. Criteria for selection of both paid personnel and volunteers must include a potential for good service attitudes.
  2. All staff must be amenable to learning.
G. Continue your commitment to training.
  1. Our technology is constantly changing, and we need to make sure we can help our users learn to use it.
  2. Our users are changing constantly as well, so our training of them will be continual.
H. Ensure communications are well-established.
  1. Patrons are aware of policies, procedures, and all services.
  2. Signs, newsletters, posters, etc., dealing with the library's services are clear, concise, and useful.
I. Follow up on execution.
  1. Make changes to processes and/or practices that are not working.
  2. Implement new plans.

J. Evaluate.
  1. Evaluate what went wrong and make changes.
  2. Reinforce the positive and applaud success.

IV. Good Customer Service Is Critical to Repeat Use
  A. Provide staff with the authority to bend policies using their good judgment so that the customer finds value.
    1. Smile.
    2. Be polite and tactful.
  B. Perception is an all-important aspect of customer service. Users need to receive:
    1. Prompt service
    2. No hassles
    3. Competent assistance
    4. Convenient hours and locations
    5. Value

V. Conclusion
  A. Libraries can be confusing and intimidating; we have a responsibility to use our expertise to connect our users with the appropriate materials and services.
  B. Suggested goals of customer service:
    1. Welcome library users and keep them feeling welcome and comfortable in the library.
    2. Determine the patrons' information needs.
    3. Match the library's resources with the users' needs in a timely fashion.
    4. Register borrowers and circulate materials in a consistent, understanding, knowledgeable, and informed fashion.
    5. Have the departing patron want to continue to use the library's services on a regular basis and to become a library supporter in the community.

Interacting with Patrons

As with all social or professional interaction, demeanor is extremely important. Demeanor is defined as the way a person looks, speaks, and acts; one's manner of behavior toward others; a personal mode of expressing attitude. Nonverbal demeanor conveys attitude via facial expressions and posture just as the tone of voice and the choice of words affect a message.

In public service institutions such as the library, it is imperative that every staff–patron interaction is a positive one for the patron. A friendly, helpful demeanor can often ensure a positive experience even when the message conveyed is not a pleasant one.

Staff members are expected to act in a friendly, helpful manner to ensure that the patron will walk away feeling that his or her experience with the library has been a positive one.

While at work, each staff member acts as the representative of the library for each person or group with whom he or she comes in contact.

The impression made on the patron profoundly affects the library's image and ongoing support.

In addition to demeanor, it is vital that library staff members treat patrons in an ethical manner. The needs and requests of library patrons must always be taken seriously and treated with respect. Equal consideration and treatment will be given to users within established guidelines and in a nonjudgmental environment.

All interactions and transactions between a library patron or group of patrons and the library will be considered confidential and will be discussed only in a professional context (such matters include, but are not limited to, registration information, materials selection, loan transaction records, reference questions, patron card status, etc.). Staff members should remember that, although the temptation to discuss or share difficult transactions at the public desk is great, such discussion should be limited to private offices, and should only be held in an effort to assist the patron. Staff members should not offer personal opinions or advice in answer to queries, but should always follow the established library practice.

Figures 8.10, 8.11, and 8.12 are useful during the training to spark discussions among the participants. You cannot expect staff to perform in a certain way if you do not let them know what is expected. It is important in training to provide sample situations so participants can think about how they would apply the policy in given situations.

Figure 8.10. Customer Service Training Handout 2: Positive Operating Procedures

General Policies

1. Be punctual. Service commences at the advertised hour we open. Phones should be answered and workstations staffed when the library opens to the public.

2. Smile.

3. Greet the patron. Acknowledge the patron's presence by looking up and making eye contact or by greeting them verbally.

4. Look up and around periodically. Being helpful to patrons takes precedence over desk work; patrons should not be led to think otherwise.

5. Conduct transactions in a helpful, pleasant tone of voice. Keep any impatience, annoyance, or implication of ignorance from your voice. Pretend it is their first visit to the library (if not, it may be their last). It is always better to presume that the patron is unfamiliar with the library.

6. Unless a specific discipline problem arises, do not reprimand or scold patrons.

7. Be jargon free when talking to library patrons.
   a. Avoid library and computer jargon or abbreviations that may be meaningless to the patron (for example, "circulation," "delinquency").
   b. Explain to the patron what procedure you will be following if it is not readily apparent (for example, "I will be contacting another library for the book that you want; it may take several days. We will notify you when it comes in").

(Continued)

Figure 8.10. Customer Service Training Handout 2: Positive Operating Procedures *(Continued)*

Department-Specific Policies

Children's Library

1. If a book is not on the shelf, check the computer, then trucks of books to be shelved; offer to reserve the book. Suggest a similar book that is in.

2. If you cannot answer a particular question, refer the patron to the adult department. Call ahead to alert them that the child has asked for help in the Children's Library already.

Circulation Department

1. If a patron forgets his or her card, offer to look it up. Remind the patron that it is important to carry their card for the next time.

2. If the patron comes up delinquent, suggest some options:

    a. Renew overdue materials if patron says they are at home.

    b. Offer to hold the items for three days so patron can clear delinquency.

    c. Offer to copy materials if only a few pages are needed.

    d. If the patron has a stop on his or her card, offer a shorter loan period if he or she has an urgent need for the material.

Adult Reference Desk

1. Conduct a proper reference interview. Make sure that you give the patron what he or she wants, which is not necessarily what was asked for.

    a. Clarify what the person really needs.

    b. Follow up whenever possible with "Did you find what you were looking for?" or "May I help you further?"

    c. Never let the patron leave without an answer to his or her question or without a referral to another source. The words "We don't have that here" should always be followed by "but I'll see if I can locate it for you elsewhere."
        1) Offer to help with all equipment.
        2) Offer to reserve materials.
        3) Offer interlibrary loan, or downloading materials if possible.
        4) Offer to fill in an order form for a new title.
        5) Call another library for information if appropriate.
        6) Give the patron a referral to someone who can answer the question.
        7) Never point. Always go to the shelf, online public access catalog (OPAC) etc., with the patron.

Figure 8.11. Customer Service Training Handout 3: Applying Customer Service Techniques to Customer Service Goals

Goal	Staff Expectation	Special Considerations
To welcome the library user	To direct patrons to appropriate location, approaching them in a friendly, courteous manner	Libraries can be confusing and intimidating, especially to people with little or no library experience, so be patient and courteous in providing service. Patrons expect immediate satisfaction. If it is not possible to give it to them, be sure to make the referral in a very helpful manner.
To determine the patron's information needs	Everyone on staff should be knowledgeable about the location of materials. Patrons should be directed to the staff member best able to help them, in light of the subject and the depth of the question.	Many patrons have only a vague awareness of what they want, or they ask for something other than what they really want, so queries must be made politely to understand the exact information need. Patrons are not aware of the differences in levels of training of support staff and librarians, so they must be assured that they are getting the "expert." A librarian with extensive reference interview experience can save much time and frustration for patrons and staff.
To match the library's resources with the user's needs in a timely fashion	The staff member should link the user with the resource. If they are able to, they should teach users to help themselves. If a transaction is not possible with the collection, then the staff member should make arrangements for the patron.	Ultimately, the patron will decide which materials to use. The staff member's role is to suggest appropriate resources.
To register borrowers and circulate materials in a consistent and informed fashion	The staff must know the library's procedures and policies, as well as have thorough familiarity with the library's circulation system. In addition, staff members need to maintain a friendly, helpful, positive, and tactful posture during patron transactions.	A good level of cooperation and trust must be developed among the staff so they can support one another in any given situation.

	Figure 8.12. Customer Service Training Handout 4: Practicing Customer Service Skills	
Situation	**Scenario**	**Response**
Child patron with poor track record	A child, age ten, comes to the desk to check out some books. His mother is standing behind him with an unpleasant look on her face. The child does not have his card with him. You look it up on the computer to find that he has five different cards registered to him. He is also blocked from checking out more materials because he has not returned his other books.	
Fees for library equipment	A college-age customer comes to you for help. He does not have any money but needs to copy some material. Each page costs ten cents. What can you do to help?	
New borrower	A woman comes into the library and she wants to check out materials. However, she does not have a library card or proof of identification with her. What do you do?	
Checking out reference materials	A student arrives at your desk and desperately needs to take home a reference book for a term paper due in the morning. He promises to have the book back at 8 a.m. You allow the reference book out, but he does not return it at 8 a.m. The student doesn't answer the phone when you call, and the book does not come back until 4 p.m. How do you handle this situation?	
Lost materials	The patron insisted that a book that is outstanding on his card has been returned. You verify that the shelves have been searched and the book is not in the library. What do you do?	

QUALITY SERVICE CONSIDERATIONS

Library's Perspective

- Customers should never be inconvenienced because of policies that are known only to employees.
- A customer should not have to request or complain to several employees before having it resolved.
- Quality service means never having to say "That's not my job."
- Customers cannot be satisfied until they are not dissatisfied. Your first service priority should be to eliminate, as much as possible, causes of customer dissatisfaction.
- Quality is the result of a systematic approach that takes time, attention, and effort. It is consistent.

Customers' Criteria for Service

- Reliability
- Responsiveness
- Authority
- Empathy
- Physical appearance of the facility

Staff Development and Technology

Libraries deal with changes in providing information almost on a daily basis. Patrons' skills and their expectations about technology are part of this change; the second part is the advancement of technological developments. In such an environment, librarians risk being outdated unless they constantly upgrade and add to their competencies and skills. Because this information is so interwoven with technology, it is absolutely essential that every librarian become savvy about information technology. Library professionals have been at the forefront of information technology, so it stands to reason that using this technology for educational purposes has become a very popular alternative. The digital revolution has created new learning opportunities, including webinars, blogs, e-journals, listservs, and discussion groups. For those completing their professional degree, certain courses will expose them to all of the current practices, but busy working librarians likely do not have the time for this formal process. So what is one to do?

Learning about Current Technology

First, staff members should consider the ways in which they learn best. If it is indeed through course work, then they should work with the director to see whether this option is available. Some might recognize that they can learn on their own through exploration of resources available online, and hence select this option. Trying out options to see what would be useful during daily work certainly falls in the realm of staff development. Before choosing a program, one should be sure the program's curriculum is sound and that the design is suitable for a particular learning style.

Collaboration and learning from one another is also another way to develop a staff, while simultaneously managing the changes in technology. With the assistance of our colleagues, we can discover some sources that we might not have found on our own. In some cases, these sources can help us to do our jobs better and more efficiently.

Professional companies are offering e-learning because it makes their programs much more accessible to more people simultaneously. It also makes the training one-to-one learning, and the student is able to try out materials and, in some cases, "fail" in private without the embarrassment that can result in a traditional classroom.

Technology literacy is a necessity in order to survive in today's digital environment. The use of social software demands a new set of skills for the librarian. The use of these tools can, in fact, save time. They recognize what interests you, identify similar resources, and make information available to use with minimal initial effort. Library staff should try out as many technologies as they can. Some will be useful and interesting; others will be efficient and have the potential to assist them with their daily work. Librarians will want to find out which technologies patrons are using on a regular basis. This will help staff communicate with them in a manner in which they are accustomed, and they will likely be more receptive. As has been discussed, good communication is a way to improve marketing for all of the library's resources and services.

Examples of Current Technological Tools

Web 2.0

The term "Web 2.0" is commonly associated with web applications that facilitate interactive information sharing. In short, this means that this type of site allows its users to interact with other users on the system. It also allows changes to be made to the pages instead of just retrieving information. Some common examples of Web 2.0 services include the social-networking sites, video-sharing sites, wikis, and blogs.

The following are two resources that librarians can use to learn about these technologies. I am certain that more will be developed as time goes on.

- Learning 2.0/The 23 Things: This is a program designed to encourage staff to explore new technologies. (http://plcmcl2-about.blogspot.com/)

- Five Weeks to a Social Library: This is an online course devoted to teaching librarians about social software and how to use it in their libraries. (http://www.sociallibraries.com/course/)

Really Simple Syndication (RSS) Feeds

RSS feeds allow you to collect news that is of interest to you from several sources. It puts the news in one place so you do not have to visit many websites. This can be installed on your computer, or it can be accessed through the web. Some users refer to RSS as Rich Site Summary because of the nature of the product. The following are some examples.

- Google Reader (http://reader.google.com): This system will capture your favorite websites and send them in an e-mail to you so that you do not have to visit all of the sites.

- Bloglines (http://bloglines.com): This free newsletter is easy to learn to use.
- Live Bookmarks (http://support.mozilla.com): This treats RSS feeds in real time. It simplifies your searching the web by collecting your favorites and transmitting them to you.

Current Awareness Services

These are services that make specific information available through a variety of means, such as e-mail and RSS. Examples include the following.

- Table of Contents (TOC) Alerts: This is a useful way to identify articles of interest; tables of contents are e-mailed to the user each time a new issue of a journal is published.
- Database Search Alerts: This is a system that sends you a notification when new articles have been added to a database from which you have saved a search. These can be set up to run automatically, or at a defined period of time.
- Search Engine Results Alerts: This gathers information from Google, blogs, and news searches. Check out http://www.google.com/alerts.
- Google Alerts: This site looks for Google search results up to once per day.

Web Change Detection Tools

This is a way to detect pages that are not frequently updated. They are usually for sites that you would not visit on a daily basis. Some of these systems may require a registration procedure. Here are two examples:

- Watch That Page (http://www.watchthatpage.com)
- Notify Me (http://www.notifyme.com)

Social Bookmarking

This is a good tool to use to discover new trends and web pages. It is also useful to see what bookmarks other people collect online. An example is Delicious (http://www.delicious.com). This will assist the librarian to keep in tune with what the patrons are using. The systems are a good way of contacting people to let them know what is happening at the library and to ask for input. While new, more and more libraries are beginning to use these as part of their overall marketing strategy.

Social Networks

These are online "communities." Software enables online meetings, collaboration, and sharing among those registered as members. More and more people are using these as a major communications tool. Professional sites include the following:

- Linkedin (http://www.linkedin.com)
- Ning (http://www.ning.com/)
- Squidoo (http://www.squidoo.com/)

General sites include the following:

- Facebook (http://www.facebook.com)
- Flickr (http://www.flickr.com)
- Twitter (http://www.twitter.com)

Some of the material for this section on social networking was selected from "Keeping Up to Speed: Tools to Help You Stay Current," by Daniela Solomon in *Connecticut Libraries*, October 2009, p. 6.

Web Conferencing Tools and Technology

This is one of the technologies that make it possible for librarians to participate in staff development activities without leaving the library. This technology has greatly increased the quantity and quality of the options that are available for the purpose of continuing education. Web conferencing provides the user with the ability to access conferencing and collaboration features along with the ability to talk, present, and demonstrate to an online audience. This is generally used to hold group meetings or live presentations via the Internet. Participants sit at their own computers and use the Internet to participate in the meeting.

One key feature of this particular technology that makes it very efficient is that it is accessible either on the web or through downloadable software. This technology includes real-time, text-based chats, so that communication among participants is facilitated. Screen-sharing may be another option; this provides the ability for participants to view one another's monitors. Presentation methods include PowerPoint, video, or a "whiteboard," a live annotation tool that can be used to call up pictures or diagrams in real time.

IMPORTANT QUESTIONS TO ASK ABOUT WEB CONFERENCES

- Is there a cost, or is it free?
- Is there live or streaming video?
- Voice over Internet Protocol (VoIP): Is there real-time audio communications/headphones/speakers?
- Is there a web tour?
- Is there a whiteboard with annotation that allows presenter and attendees to highlight or mark items on slide presentation?
- Text chat: Is this available to allow for a live question-and-answer period?
- Are you able to record your webcast to share and play back at any time?
- Does the system have shared file space?
- Is there technical support?

SELECTED SOFTWARE AND SERVICE PROVIDERS

- Adobe Acrobat Connect (http://www.adobe.com/products) enables document transferals and printing of files.
- Big Blue Button (http://www.bigbluebutton.org) enables usability of transferred information.
- Citrix Online (http://www.citrix.com) enables desktop visualization and networking.
- Dimdim (http://www.dimdim.com) enables sharing, document sharing, and document storage.
- Elluminate (http://www.elluminate.com) provides live virtual classrooms.
- Genesys Meeting Center (http://www.genesys.com) is an excellent tool for online communications.
- Glace (http://www.glace.com) is software for web conferencing.
- IBM Lotus Live (http://www.ibmlotus.com/live) is a web-based, security-rich e-mail system.
- IBM Lotus Sametime (http://www.ibmlotus.com/sametime) is a unified web conferencing system.
- Microsoft Office Live Meeting (http://www.microsoft/com) enables users to share and store documents as well as hold online meetings.
- Netviewer (http://www.netviewer.com) provides desktop maintenance and online conferencing.
- OmNovia Technologies (http://www.omnovia.com) provides an e-learning environment and web conferencing software.
- OpenMeetings (http://www.openmeetings.org) is software to enable online meetings and webinars.
- Oracle Beehive (http://www.oraclebeehive.com) is collaborative software that allows for team meetings and instant messaging.
- Premiere Global Services (http://www.pgi.com) is a system for global conferencing.
- Show Document (http://www.showdocument.com) allows for document sharing and storage.
- Talk Point (http://www.talkpointcommunications.com) allows for webinars and online meetings.
- Time Bridge (http://www.timebridge.com) provides a communication tool for online learning.
- WebEx (http://www.webex.com) is software for web conferences.
- WebTrain (http://www.webtrain.com) provides for online meetings and conference services.
- Yugma (http://www.yugma.com) provides a communication package for online trainings.

Evaluation as a Professional Development Tool

10

IN THIS CHAPTER:

✔ Evaluation's Role in Staff Development

✔ Aspects of Evaluation

✔ Responding to Staff Resistance to Evaluation-Based Change

Whether for profit or nonprofit, every organization needs evaluation procedures to measure its effectiveness. Performance appraisals are necessary on an annual basis, and they are best when they are developed in collaborative planning sessions between supervisors and employees. Goals and objectives must be set for the upcoming year, and the training offered should be structured around accomplishing them. In fact, the performance evaluation process may be a key to determining the ongoing needs of staff and direct the staff development coordinator in future planning. Many valuable books on the subject of performance appraisal are available, most notably Sullivan and Steuart's *Performance Analysis and Appraisal* (New York: Neal-Schuman, 1991). Some points from that book are highlighted here so that performance evaluation techniques can be tied to the evaluation process that is necessary for staff development.

Good performance evaluation will measure the individual's performance on the job in comparison with the job requirements that were listed on the job description when the employee was hired. The supervisor must be able to assess the quality of the individual's performance and recommend whether the individual is to receive a promotion, a salary increase, or special training or retraining. It is the supervisor's responsibility to understand what the employee's potential is, and how it fits into the institution's goals. Performance appraisal time may be when the director should consider whether the staff member's job description may need updating. It will, of course, depend on whether the jobs in your library are classified by union standards or local practice. Certainly this is an opportunity to begin the process, especially if the staff member is being required to take on new responsibilities due to staff changes or new technologies.

Typical standards of employee performance are quality and quantity (How well? How many?); the desired effect or impact (Has the employee completed the job? To what degree of accuracy? Were deadlines met?); and meeting standards (Was the work accomplished in cooperation with others? Has the employee been able to adapt to the needs of the job at hand?).

WHY EVALUATE?

- To determine if the needs of the participants have been met
- To determine if the needs of the organization have been met
- To justify the program
- To establish credibility
- To adapt the program if it is not functioning to meet needs

The results of performance appraisal are traditionally used to provide the employee with praise and recognition or constructive criticism and assistance. Supervisors use the exercise as a way of reinforcing organizational objectives and expectations, and they should focus on the employee's potential for improvement and development. As with any good communications process, the employee should be given a forum during this review process to express needs, concerns, and questions.

In addition to the formal process of appraisal, supervisors have other means of evaluation at their disposal. These include on-the-job observation, specific opportunities to apply training knowledge, and demonstrations to other employees. Supervisors can use Figures 10.1 and 10.2, or variations of them, when rating or evaluating employees' performance.

Figure 10.1. Supervisor's Self-Evaluation Checklist

1. What is your personal attitude about the library? Do you think your attitude affects your ability to supervise others?

2. Do you think that your immediate supervisor is competent?

3. Are you performing your administrative/supervisory functions well?

4. When was the last time you appraised your own performance? Were you objective and honest with yourself?

5. When was the last time you were evaluated by your supervisor? Did you agree with the evaluation?

6. Do your subordinates respect your leadership and technical capabilities?

7. What is your relationship with other supervisors in the library?

8. Do you readily accept new responsibilities?

9. Are you open-minded about suggestions for improvements?

10. Is there any reason to believe that your work is ineffective or not up to standard?

11. Do you participate in opportunities for continuing education?

12. Are you considered to possess a high degree of integrity?

Figure 10.2. Checklist for Rating Employees	
1. Technical Ability	6. Attendance/Punctuality
a. Understands all phases of work	a. Has a minimal absentee record
b. Knows how to use all equipment	b. Is flexible in scheduling
c. Has knowledge of all operations	c. Calls in when ill
d. Can detect own errors	d. Starts and finishes on time consistently
e. Can take corrective action	e. Reports promptly to work after break or lunch
f. Communicates well	
2. Dependability	7. Attention to Work Environment
a. Follows instructions	a. Has a neat workstation
b. Meets most deadlines	b. Properly disposes of trash and recycles
c. Cross-checks results	c. Stores materials carefully
d. Is flexible with scheduling	d. Keeps equipment in good order
	e. Observes safety rules
3. Personality	8. Adaptability
a. Gets along well with other workers	a. Is supportive of changes
b. Is willing to help others	b. Learns new methods and equipment
c. Is cooperative	c. Shows a willingness to be retrained
d. Attempts to resolve disputes quickly	d. Respects authority
4. Productivity	9. Potential
a. Maintains a good level of output	a. Seeks to be recognized for expertise
b. Has a minimum of wasted effort	b. Studies and trains for promotion
c. Revises methods that cause problems or errors	c. Trains or leads others
	d. Is motivated
5. Attitude	10. Commitment
a. Overcomes work difficulties	a. To the organization
b. Is a good team worker	b. To the profession
c. Respects supervisors	
d. Willing to train others	
e. Respects and appreciates customers and their needs	

Evaluation's Role in Staff Development

In particular, evaluation should be done as projects are in progress; ongoing feedback helps keep projects on the right track. Staff development programs are certainly included in this category. Managers use evaluation to measure the effectiveness of each training session, as well as of the overall program, on a semiannual basis. They should be looking at how well the program is able to transfer information from the trainer(s) to the participants and what differences in operations have resulted from the training. All trainers will also want to evaluate how well they taught the necessary information. As the library's administrator, you are going to want to keep yourself aware of the work of all of the trainers. You will want to judge them from a formal standpoint on how they transferred data and whether employees were then able to apply their newly acquired knowledge. You will want to pay careful attention to employee feedback on the training to evaluate whether particular trainers are in tune with the needs of the participants. Evaluation of the trainer needs to be done on a serious level by the administrator to assess whether he or she has effectively met the course objectives. Good trainers will be evaluating themselves and should be willing to share their thoughts with you. Trainers can word questions on written evaluations to provide some of this much needed feedback. For example, participants could be asked to answer yes or no to questions such as:

- "Did the trainer use clear examples?"
- "Was each point covered with enough detail?"
- "Did the trainer hold your interest?"

The more detailed the questions, the more specific will be the data that you have to improve further efforts. We need to keep in mind that good, overall evaluation procedures will make your programs more effective and will increase not only levels of knowledge but also the library's credibility.

Aspects of Evaluation

Evaluations provide the means by which we are able to judge the success of our training program. Training evaluation comprises three primary aspects. The first is the pre-course entry evaluation, which can zero in on the training or knowledge level of the group on any particular subject. This provides the basis for the session. It is not necessarily the needs assessment that was discussed earlier, but certainly the picture that one is able to derive from that process is helpful prior to developing the program. Simply stated, it might contain a few questions that the trainer asks his or her audience before getting into the course material. For example, the trainer might ask, "How many of you have had an unpleasant experience at a store recently?" and then ask for a show of hands. A follow-up question—such as "What was your reaction?" or "Will you go back to that store?"—can elicit comments and give the trainer some insight into whether the participants are able to distinguish between good and bad customer service. This exercise can be viewed as a pretest and will give the trainer important information on the audience's background, attitudes, and experiences and will launch the workshop.

Second, continuing course evaluation monitors conditions that can be adjusted or changed as necessary while the workshop is being held. These conditions include the pace at which the workshop is being offered; the level of the material that is being used; the quality of any audiovisual aids (Are they clear? Are they focused?); the amount of participation from the audience (Are they responding? Asking questions? Nodding in agreement?); and the course logistics (room temperature, break times, seating arrangements).

Finally, the post-course evaluation views the overall effectiveness of the training program. This should be done as soon as possible after the program is complete so that the information is fresh, but it should also be done after those trained have been able to apply their newly learned skills.

When evaluating participant reactions, you should be careful to pay attention to adverse reactions to the facilities and room arrangements. Although not directly associated with the training program itself, these factors can affect the participants' attitudes toward the program. Anything that can be done to make the participants comfortable will aid in their capacity to learn. Program content should be evaluated in terms of coverage of the topic, on whether it met the objectives of the course, and whether it increased the participants' knowledge. One of the best means of evaluating content is through the use of a questionnaire that is rated on a scale. This type of evaluation of content is important to improve program material. Figure 10.3 gives you some ideas regarding what factors to consider when evaluating a training program.

Administrators, and in some cases trainers, are also going to need to evaluate the knowledge gain and behavioral changes. Written and oral tests are sometimes appropriate to see whether people actually learned the material that was presented; however, the best results can be gained from performance testing, which goes a step beyond finding out if the

Figure 10.3. Employee Evaluation

The purpose of the employee evaluation is to take a personal inventory of the individual, pinpointing both strengths and weaknesses. The employee and the supervisor should be able to reach some consensus and should develop a practical empowerment program that includes expectations and goals. All categories should be discussed.

Categories of Judgment

1. Accuracy: How much supervision is required?
2. Alertness: What is the ability to learn and understand?
3. Creativity: Does the person have a talent for having new ideas and for finding new and better ways of doing things?
4. Personality: Is the person suited to the job, and how does he or she relate to customers, other employees, supervisors?
5. Attendance: Is the employee punctual and reliable?
6. Housekeeping: Is the work area clean and orderly?
7. Dependability: Are required jobs done well with a minimum of supervision?
8. Job knowledge: Does the employee have information concerning duties necessary to perform the job satisfactorily?
9. Productivity: How much does the employee produce in a given day?
10. Drive: Is there a desire to attain goals?

METHODS OF EVALUATION

Quantitative:
- Number of sessions
- Number of people trained
- Which program attracted the most people?

Participants' reaction to training:
- Instruction
- Content
- Method
- Organization

Learning:
- Achievement of objectives
- Verification of competency
- Tests and practice sessions

Performance measures:
- Individual performance
- Application to on-the-job situations
- Behavioral changes/results

Results:
- Impact of the training on patrons
- Organizational effectiveness

participants learned the material. Performance testing evaluates if they are using it in a particular manner.

Evaluating behavior changes is a means to determine the distinction between learning and performing. This is best done by comparing levels of performance to performance levels preceding the trainings. Ultimately, the most critical evaluation is to see the impact from the individual training on the overall organization.

Once the training programs and the evaluation process are completed, the supervisor or staff development coordinator should be ready to report the results of the training process to those at all levels of concern in the organization, and indeed outside it. Reporting results helps clarify training skills and procedures and also can aid the participants in determining additional training needs. Written reports should be clear and to the point. They should include the needs that you expect to be met after the training session; a summary of the training that was offered; a statement that answers the question "Were the needs met?", and an identification of additional training needs.

Once your library has a staff development program in place, it will become natural for the evaluation of staff performance to be enhanced by evaluating the actual results of the program. It is crucial to remember that one of the best ways of getting people to participate is to make them feel that they are part of the larger organization. The supervisor's evaluation is key in this area. Helping people to be perceived as part of the organization is so important. As administrators, we are not above the need to be evaluated, and we must take the time to reflect on our own strengths and weaknesses (see Figure 10.4). Our involvement in the process may just be the spark that will make other staff members enthusiastic.

Figure 10.4. Overcoming Employee Resistance to Change

All managers will face employees who are finding it difficult to accept change at some time during their careers. A good method of counteracting these attitudes is to prepare for the reactions by anticipating them. Here is a list of some common reactions and attitudes:

1. Premature judgment: "Before you go any further, it won't work."
2. Cursory evaluation: Only the most obvious factors are considered; detail is ignored.
3. Self-serving assumptions: The person jumps to conclusions that he or she finds desirable, and ignores the actual facts.
4. Single-value judgment: Only one criterion is judged.
5. Either/or: Oversimplified judgment instead of value is used to evaluate change.
6. Inaccurate value scales: An inaccurate scale of values is used to evaluate change.
7. Sweeping generalizations: Stereotypes are offered of people, things, and ideas without regard to actual facts.
8. Semantic approach: Certain words or phrases are used to cause an emotional response that could result in unfortunate, inconclusive, or inadequate judging of facts.

The supervisor who can anticipate the employees' responses might be able to counteract the negatives at the outset and will be better able to overcome resistance.

Responding to Staff Resistance to Evaluation-Based Change

Any new innovation—whether it is a change in the way a task is approached, a new piece of equipment to do the job, a change to an electronic or CD-ROM database instead of hard copy—will be met with some resistance by a few staff members. It is human nature to resist change; we are comfortable with that which is familiar. In every workplace, we will always have those who say, "We always have done it that way, so why change?" or "We tried that and it did not work."

It is the responsibility of the library director to provide the staff, and in some cases, the board of directors, all of the pros and cons of changes. The director should anticipate what some negative reactions might be (see Figure 10.5) and prepare arguments to counter them. When people are able to understand the benefits or even the necessity of making the change, their reactions will ultimately overcome the negatives and the resistance. Many people are negative when they do not understand the rationale behind the change, are not able to envision the benefits, or fear that their tasks may become more difficult. In fact, they may discover that new methods of working can eliminate some tedious and repetitive aspects of their work. They often will become the strongest supporters of the change after you take the time to explain things and ask them to help you implement the changes.

Figure 10.5. Training Program Evaluation

Successful Staff Development

Please rate the following on a scale of 1 to 5, with 1 being the lowest and 5 the highest.

1. Content of materials   _____
2. Handouts   _____
3. Style of delivery   _____
4. Adequate time   _____
5. Questions answered   _____
6. Workshop expectations met   _____
7. Other   _____

Comments:

_____

_____

_____

_____

_____

Rewarding Effective Performance

Salary increases and monetary and fringe benefits are important to everyone, but they certainly are not the only reason people become motivated to do their best on the job. Both experience and research indicate that most people need to feel positive about the job they are doing. People who feel capable and competent in performing their jobs will be highly motivated to continue to perform them well. It is important that supervisors encourage these feelings of competence. Every good manager should be aware of the potential benefits of praise and positive feedback. These are ways to inspire and motivate people, who like to know that their efforts, as well as the results of these efforts, are truly appreciated. The praise must be consistent with the expectations that the supervisor has for the employee, or it becomes quite easy for the employee to shrug off the praise as inconsequential. On the other hand, it is also true that most people want to know when they are not performing properly, but they want to know in a way that does not force them to swallow their pride or lose self-respect. If criticized before other staff members or not given the chance to save face, they may become resentful; rather than improving the employee's performance, the feedback may only worsen it. Giving effective criticism is a valuable skill that every supervisor should develop as an important part of management responsibilities. As crucial as it is to give someone a pat on the back, other kinds of recognition are valuable as well. Employees should be able to accrue benefits from their achievements and from the satisfactory acceptance of particular responsibilities.

Recognition versus Promotion

Recognition comes in many forms. Beyond simple praise, employees should be encouraged, when appropriate, to assume more challenging work within the library. Promotions are not always possible, but some symbols of the new status often work as well and can be acquired for very little or no money. A change in title, a new name badge, and the relocation of work space are a few examples of what might be included within this realm of possibilities.

WHY RECOGNIZE EMPLOYEES' ACHIEVEMENTS?

- People need confirmation of their successes.
- Performance can be improved by status symbols and awards.
- External recognition reinforces one's faith in one's own performance.

Any praise or rewards given to employees should be additional recognition rather than a substitute for raises or promotions due the employee. Many times, however, library administrators do not have control of the funding for these positions. The governing body may decide that no raises are to be given, and our hands are tied insofar as giving employees much needed pay increases. We must remain sensitive to this scenario and recognize that giving an employee a certificate for good work under these circumstances most likely will not be appreciated. On the other hand, if the reward is made in addition to the other raises, vacation days, or similar incentives that are due the employee, it can do wonders. The recognition has to be a sign of appreciation rather than a substitute for a raise for it to be effective.

Recognition and Internal Marketing

Recognition is actually the final piece of an internal marketing strategy that can be used to enhance the pride and the commitment of the employee within the organization. Employees should realize that their achievements will bring pride and recognition to the library as well as themselves and that they are appreciated for this. This awareness of their personal contributions links the employees to the tradition and the heritage of the library. In addition, the proper use of the recognition of one employee will create pride in all staff members. They will feel good to know that their library employs the best. Recognition has another great, hidden benefit: nothing generates success more than success. Recognition can encourage further creativity and productivity.

If we want employees to strive for excellence, we must set the standards for that excellence. We must praise their achievements and contributions, and ensure that these individuals are appreciated by their colleagues and the decision makers alike. Include the recognition in a newspaper, share it at a staff meeting, and/or hold celebrations. Monetary remuneration is important, and the staff member's position and salary should reflect his or her contribution to the organization. However, we should not overlook the human satisfaction employees receive when we commend them for a job well done.

The administration participates in internal marketing when it exhibits care through the personal environment that is provided for the staff. While work areas do not need to be luxurious, they should be clean, safe, comfortable, and reasonably attractive. The result is that when concern is shown to employees, it influences how they feel about their organization.

An administrator who wants to have a successful organization is wise to develop an internal marketing program that will allow for the integration of attitude and efforts. This process will contribute to the achievement of the library's goals. Our responsibility is to make organizations the very best that they can be. To do so, I believe we must put our employees first. Then our patrons will receive a level of service that comes from the heart, and they are able to appreciate its value even more.

Recognition Strategies

Many strategies for providing recognition exist. One of the simplest ways is to convey recognition of the achievement verbally at the time of the performance or within a reasonable time thereafter. An example might be, "Jane, you handled the public beautifully during the power outage. Many of them might have panicked in the darkness, but you kept your cool, and they followed suit. Nice work." Providing this type of recognition within earshot of other staff members, or in public, is appropriate, and the employee usually will be most appreciative of your effort to single him or her out.

Sometimes, it is effective to render recognition more than once. An achievement such as the one just mentioned might be rephrased and presented to the governing board or repeated in a newspaper article commending Jane. This provides the opportunity for others to join in the applause. At other times, it might be better to call the employee aside and commend him or her in private.

As a manager, you may find useful some reinforcement techniques for keeping employees involved and interested, and to help the staff to develop a sense of commitment to the process of staff development. First and foremost will be the sense of achievement employees feel when they are able to apply the knowledge or skill acquired from participation in a staff development program. Two other ways of providing reinforcement have already been discussed:

- Using staff members as trainers
- Finding ways, in addition to salary increases, to recognize and reward performance

In any case, a sense of achievement is most often what will provide the motivation for individuals to continue their participation, because by its very nature motivation is an internal, personal response. It cannot be provided solely by an outside influence.

In addition to communications, staff members must be helped to identify with your organization. Attractive name badges and business cards help establish this identity. Perhaps special events might warrant a staff shirt, or other identifying item. Personal contacts are also strengthened through recognition of special events in a person's life (birthday, anniversary, graduation, etc.) or the achievements of family members, genuine assistance during times of need, and social opportunities that bring the staff together to celebrate, to relax, and even to share sorrow.

WAYS TO GIVE RECOGNITION

- Handshake
- An engraved certificate or plaque
- Flowers or a small memento
- Simple thank you—oral or written
- Letter of appreciation in personnel file
- An appreciation luncheon or tea
- Pin that recognizes achievement
- Special parking place
- Public acknowledgment
- Limited edition of an item
- Business cards
- Recognition from someone with power (mayor, elected official)
- Larger work space or office
- A more challenging job as an opportunity for growth

Rewards and Motivation

Employees who feel appreciated by their organization and colleagues will be better motivated to do a more conscientious job. A little pat on the back once in a while can do wonders for productivity at no cost and with little effort. Recognition provides staff with security and a sense of belonging, and it improves overall morale.

Rewards are important because they provide psychological motivation for the staff. Once good behaviors have been established, a relatively small amount of reinforcement will help maintain their momentum. Reinforcement is more powerful the more immediate it is, and continuous reinforcement maintains good behavior. Both excellence and progress should be recognized.

Managers can purchase several kinds of items that are intended to provide recognition. They are inspiring and attractive, but their cost may be out of reach for most library budgets. The recognition gift does not need to be expensive in order to be effective, however. In fact, many have no cost at all. The most important thing is that the item is appropriate for the given situation and for the particular employee who is receiving it. Anything personalized with the name, date, and occasion is always valued.

Manager's Role

While it marks achievement, recognition has the added potential of being the first step in another cycle of achievement. Staff development keeps people from burning out, and it is a never-ending process. If we are going to deliver quality services, we must support this process on an ongoing basis. Staff development is an investment in our futures; it should be a library priority, but must also be a shared responsibility between the employer and the employee. The most difficult thing about effective management is that you must keep on doing it to be effective, and you must teach others in a supervisory position to do it as well.

Those who are in management must remember that change begins with us. Management is a difficult job, and we cannot do it alone. We must surround ourselves with well-trained staff members who can help. Changing your organization is not a single, ultimate solution; it is, in fact, a never-ending process that keeps on presenting different sets of problems. Managing the process of change through effective staff development is a major part of the solution.

This book has presented some basic take-away concepts. First, in order to empower others, you must empower yourself. You, the director, must exhibit continuing development and learning, openness to new ideas, willingness to try them, and skill in melding them into the traditions and the mission of the library. Second, you must convey to your staff your firm and abiding belief that change, though inevitable, can be managed and shaped so it is a positive force rather than a confusing and negative one. It is basic to your program of staff development that you articulate constantly the truth that staff development must be a given for every member of the organization—professionals, support staff, trustees, and volunteers—and that this requirement will only increase in the decades to come.

WAYS TO RECOGNIZE EMPLOYEES

- Change in title or position
- Change in office
- Article in newspaper
- Certificate or plaque

OPPORTUNITIES TO PROVIDE RECOGNITION

- Achievement of a particular goal
- Completing a project
- Submission of cost-savings suggestions
- Year of perfect attendance
- Extensive on-time record
- Community service
- Professional service
- Suggestion of a new way to provide a service or perform a routine task
- Feedback from a user about a staff member
- Completion of formal training
- Leadership during a crisis

Resource Directory

IN THIS CHAPTER:

✔ Facts about Libraries

✔ Library Journals

✔ Library Acronyms

✔ National Resource Directory

✔ Online Sources

✔ People Resources

✔ Suggested Readings

✔ Tools for Trainers and Recognition Resources

Library administrators should be members of their state and regional associations, as well as of the American (or Canadian) Library Association. If your library is of a special nature, you would, of course, align with them as well. This may be the Special Libraries Association, or Medical Library Association, or a special division for music, law, or other specific subjects. They should also be members of specific sections or roundtables that are specific to the type of library. In addition to holding memberships themselves, administrators should encourage membership among eligible employees. Many libraries are able to include membership dues as a legitimate professional development expense, and should do so if they are able. Furthermore, all staff should be encouraged to participate fully in these associations, attend their meetings and conferences, and serve on various committees and task forces. These are excellent opportunities to broaden staff expertise and knowledge, often at an incredibly reasonable cost.

Membership and networking with other organizations in the community is another opportunity that library administrators should not overlook as a way of encouraging professional growth. Participation in the Chamber of Commerce of your town allows you to join in the seminars they offer. A hidden advantage of such membership is the networking that you will be able to do with other members of the business community. You might then be able to find out what types of training they are doing and perhaps piggyback onto it. An organization may see this as a way to make an appropriate donation to the library. As another advantage, they might lend an executive for a day so the person can be a volunteer trainer. Other civic-minded organizations that are good investments for membership are Rotary Clubs, Kiwanis, and Lions. These groups, too, can provide support and assistance to your staff development program. Another important part of this approach is what our libraries are able to do for these organizations. Our staffs have specialized skills and can provide services that these groups may not be able to get elsewhere. We also have meeting rooms and materials that we lend. The opportunities for you to create partnerships with them are there, and in my experience, they are worth the effort.

Again, if your library has a specialty, it would behoove you to seek out related groups that may be in the city or on the campus.

These organizations have fine recommendations for staff development, and equally respected reputations:

American Management Association
135 West 50th Street
New York, New York 10020-1201

> This association sponsors forums worldwide and also publishes books and program materials that help administrators promote the development and growth of staffs.

Institute of Museum and Library Services
1800 M Street, NW
Washington, DC 20036

> This federal resource can provide information on libraries and grants available. It can also refer you to the state library in your state.

International City/County Management Association (ICMA)
777 North Capitol Street NE, Suite 500
Washington, DC 20002-4201

> This association specializes in working with county and municipal employees. They offer many courses and training seminars.

Non-Profit Management Association
315 West 9th Street, Suite 1100
Los Angeles, CA 90015

> This association provides networking for individuals who work in nonprofit areas.

Facts about Libraries

The following information has been compiled from a variety of sources about libraries. These sources include the American Library Association (http://www.ala.org), the National Center for Educational Statistics (http://nces.ed.gov), the Institute of Education Sciences (http://www.ies.gov), the U.S. Department of Education (http://www.ed.gov), and the Institute of Museum and Library Services (http://www.imls.org). The information available from these websites reveals the following information concerning U.S. libraries:

- There are over 16,500 public libraries. All colleges have libraries that support their curriculum, as do most schools.

- Nearly two-thirds of all Americans have active library cards.

- Almost one-half of all citizens use libraries for educational purposes.

- Almost one-half of all citizens use libraries for entertainment purposes.

- Nine out of ten Americans believe that libraries are dynamic places, and that they have contributed to the success of their school, work, and/or business.

Libraries have also been credited with helping start businesses, assisting people in finding employment, and in helping workers to be more productive on their jobs. In fact, a survey in one state revealed that the total direct and indirect financial return for every dollar invested returned nearly four and one-half dollars.

Library Journals

All good library administrators keep themselves abreast of the latest developments in the field by reading a variety of publications that are produced for our profession. These should include *American Libraries*, *Library Administration and Management*, *Library Journal*, and your state and regional publications as well. In addition, these sources are especially helpful:

Training and Development Journal
American Society of Training and Development
1640 King Street, Box 1443
Alexandria, VA 22331

Workforce Training News
Enterprise Communications
1483 Chain Bridge Road #202
McLean, VA 22101

Working Together
Dartneil Corp.
4469 Ravenswood Avenue
Chicago, IL 60640

Library Acronyms

The following list (compiled from research and the website of the American Library Association, http://www.ala.com) includes library and related groups that are sources of help for continuing education as well as acronyms that all librarians should know. It should be noted that many of the associations offer workshops and other trainings that can be incorporated into the library's own staff development plan. They are terms that may be used by trainers or incorporated into written documents. Depending on the training topic, the trainer may select from these and develop a handout that is appropriate for their session.

AASL: American Association of School Libraries; a division of ALA serving school library media specialists.

AASLH: American Association for State and Local History.

ACRL: Association of College & Research Libraries; a division of ALA for academic and research libraries, including large public libraries.

ADA: Americans with Disabilities Act; federal legislation to protect the rights of citizens with disabilities.

AECT: Association for Educational Communications and Technology; provides leadership in educational communications and technology by linking professionals who hold a common interest in the use of educational technology and its application to the learning process.

ALA: American Library Association; the oldest and largest organization of librarians and libraries in the country, with more than 30,000 members. ALA provides leadership for development, promotion, and improvement of library and information services and the profession of librarianship in order to enhance learning and ensure access to information for all.

ALCTS: Association for Library Collections & Technical Services; a division of ALA for professionals involved with building and organizing collections.

ALSC: Association for Library Service to Children; a division of ALA for professionals who work with children.

ALTA: Association of Library Trustees and Advocates; a division of ALA for those who are board members/trustees and library advocates.

ANSI: American National Standards Institute; this is a private, non-profit organization that administers and coordinates the U.S. voluntary standardization and conformity assessment system.

ANSI/NISO Z 39.50: This is the protocol that defines a standard method for two computers to communicate for the purpose of information retrieval.

ASCII: American Standard Code Information Interchange; a standard format for computer language.

ASCLA: Association for Specialized and Cooperative Library Agencies; again, a division of ALA that is a resource for cooperative agencies.

ASIST: American Society for Information Science and Technology; a professional organization for those concerned with the design, management, and use of information systems and technology.

CE: Continuing Education; refers to advanced training in a profession (not leading to a degree) to learn new skills or keep abreast of developments in the field.

CEU: Continuing Education Unit; one CEU is equal to one hour of instruction or contact time. CEUs are required for public school educators, including library media specialists. Some states and academic institutions also require them.

CIP: Cataloging in Publication; the cataloging information that is located on the verso of the title page of a book or other type of publication.

CLEC: Continuing Library Education Certificates; some states have a program that provides certificates for those who have completed workshops.

CLENE: Continuing Library Education Network Exchange; a roundtable of the American Library Association that brings together librarians from all over the country so they can exchange information and training ideas.

CNI: Coalition for Networked Information; dedicated to supporting the transformative promise of networked information technology for the advancement of scholarly communication and the enrichment of intellectual productivity.

COSLINE: Council of State Library Agencies in the Northeast; brings together the members of the state libraries for networking purposes.

DBMS: Database Management System.

DDC: Dewey Decimal Classification; the classification system that is used by most public libraries.

ERP: Effective Reference Performance; advance training in conducting reference interviews to increase the level of patron satisfaction.

ESEA: Elementary and Secondary Education Act; federal act that provides funds for educational programs, including library materials in the school library media centers.

FAQs: Frequently Asked Questions; many websites and discussion lists have FAQs to provide answers to common questions.

FOL: Friends of the Library are advocacy groups that can be developed for any kind of library.

FOLUSA: Friends of the Library USA is affiliated with ALA and is a resource to all local Friends groups.

FTP: File Transfer Protocol; defines how one computer transfers files to another computer.

GODORT: Government Documents Roundtable is a roundtable of ALA for those who work with government documents.

GPO: Government Printing Office. The U.S. government prints and sells books, reports, and materials that are produced by government agencies. Many are also available electronically. This is a tremendous resource for adding materials for workshops.

GUI: Graphical User Interface; allows computer users to "point and click" with a mouse to navigate on a PC.

HTML: Hypertext Markup Language; a programming code to create a hyperlinked World Wide Web document.

HTTP: Hypertext Transfer Protocol; the portion of a Web address that signifies that a document was created in HTML.

IFLA: International Federation of Library Associations and Institutions; the international body that represents the interests of library and information services and their users.

ILL: Interlibrary Loan is the process by which a library requests materials from, or supplies materials to, another library upon the request of a library user.

ILS: Integrated Library System.

IMLS: Institute of Museum and Library Services; the federal grant-making agency that promotes leadership, innovation, and a lifetime of learning by supporting the nation's museums and libraries, and administers LSTA funds.

IP: Internet Protocol.

IP address: This is a computer's unique numeric Internet address.

IPIG: ILL Protocol Implementers Group was formed to facilitate the use of the international ILL standard (ISO 1010 & 10161) by U.S. vendors and service providers.

ISBN: International Standard Book Number is the unique number that is assigned to every book published in this country, and many other countries. The number denotes the country of publication, the publisher, and the identity of the book.

ISDN: Integrated Services Digital Network is high-speed digital telecommunications lines that can transmit both voice and data.

ISO: International Organization for Standardization is a network of national standards institutes from 147 countries working in partnership with international organizations, governments, industry, business, and consumer representatives.

ISP: Internet Service Provider.

ISSN: International Standard Serial Number is the unique number assigned to periodicals by the LAMA: Library Administration and Management Association, the division of ALA for managers/directors.

LAN: Local Area Network; a network of computers within an institution.

LC: Library of Congress. This, of course, also serves as our national library. It is also the name of the classification system that is used by most larger libraries.

LCCN: This is the Library of Congress Card Number, which is assigned to an item by the Library of Congress, which is also a depository library.

LITA: Library and Information Technology Association is a division of the ALA that helps members who are interested in technology networks.

LSTA: Library Services and Technology Act; federal funding for libraries in several areas—technology, interlibrary cooperation, literacy, etc. The funds are filtered through the state libraries, and then on to local libraries.

LT: Library Technician.

LTA: Library Technical Assistant.

MARC: Machine Readable Cataloging. MARC records contain data in standardized format and allow conversion to automated cataloging and circulation systems.

MEDLINE: This is the online database of the National Library of Medicine.

MLS: Master's Degree in Library Science. The ALA accredits degree programs in the United States.

NCIP: NISO Circulation Interchange Protocol is a standard that defines the various transactions needed to support circulation activities among independent library systems.

NISO: National Information Standards Organization.

NLM: National Library of Medicine.

NNLM: National Network of Libraries of Medicine.

NREN: National Research and Education Network.

NUC: National Union Catalog. This is a national bibliography that is published by the Library of Congress.

OPAC: Online Public Access Catalog. This is a computer workstation for use by the public that is connected to a library's circulation system. It can be searched by author, title, library (if the library is part of a consortium), and shows an item's status.

PAC: Public Access Catalog; often used interchangeably with OPAC.

PLA: Public Library Association; the division of ALA that services public libraries.

PPP: Point to Point Protocol enables a computer to connect to the Internet.

RASD: Reference and Adult Services Division; a division of the ALA that is a resource for those who work in adult services and in reference.

RFC: Request for Comment.

RFI: Request for Information.

RFP: Request for Proposal.

RLIN: Research Libraries Information Network.

RUSA: Reference and User Services Association; a division of the ALA.

SLA: Special Libraries Association; a national association of librarians who work in special libraries.

SUDOC: Superintendent of Documents. This is the government office responsible for printing all government documents and assigning their classification numbers.

URL: Uniform Resource Locator; the address of a World Wide Web site.

WAN: Wide Area Network; electronically links computers at remote locations and allows them to exchange data.

WWW: World Wide Web.

YA: Young Adult; the common term for library users between the ages of 12 and 18.

National Resource Directory

Many national professional and research organizations serving concerned professionals and citizens are listed below. Many of these organizations focus on various issues related to culture/programming and are useful resources on particular topics.

American Association for State and Local History
http://www.aaslh.org/

American Association of Museums
http://www.aam-us.org/

American Library Association
http://www.ala.org/

Center for Arts and Culture
http://www.culturalpolicy.org/

Council on Library and Information Resources
http://www.clir.org/

Institute of Museum and Library Services
http://www.imls.org/

International Federation of Library Associations and Institutions
http://www.ifla.org/

Libraries of the Future
http://www.lff.org/

National Commission on Libraries and Information Sciences
http://www.nclis.gov/

National Endowment for the Arts
http://www.arts.gov/

National Endowment for the Humanities
http://www.neh.gov/

Special Libraries Association
http://www.sla.org/

Urban Libraries Council
http://www.urbanlibraries.org/

Online Sources

Many of these resources are totally free or offered at a very low cost.

Barnes and Noble University
http://www.universitybarnesandnoble.com

This site provides resources for online learning, especially book discussions.

FreeSkills.com

This site provides online training courses, tutorials, low cost e-learning opportunities, and a job resource list.

Intelinfo.com

This site will link you to free training courses and materials.

LearnThat.com

This is a comprehensive directory of distance learning, free online courses, and web-based training.

LearnWell.org

This site offers free courses.

LibrarySupportStaff.com

These are resources to use on the job in libraries.

Netscape Online Learning Center
http://learningcenter.netscape.com/courses/index.jsp

This site provides descriptions of online courses.

TechHowTo.com

This offers free tutorials to develop computer skills.

Tips for Success in Distance Learning
http://teleducation.nb.ca/content/pdf/English/lotw2002.pdf

This site fulfills its name; it offers tips for those who are interested in distance learning.

TrainingCenter.com

This site has courses that are available for a small fee.

WorldWideLearn.com

This is a connection to good online training sites.

YouLiveandLearn.com

This website is composed of short online tutorials and links to other information sites.

People Resources

The following organizations will be able to put you in contact with individuals who will be able to assist you as you plan staff development.

American Library Association
50 East Huron Street
Chicago, IL 60611

The Office of Personnel Resources and the Library Administration and Management Association are especially committed to issues relating to librarianship, career goals, and development.

Council of Consulting Organizations
521 5th Avenue
New York, New York 10175-3598

This is a group of consultants who work in consulting firms or are private consultants on various topics. Their expertise is extensive, but the cost may be prohibitive.

Special Libraries Association
P.O. Box 75338
Baltimore, MD 21275

This association has divisions that cover many specific subspecialties. Their website is especially helpful, with seminars and webcasts on its home page.

It is important that you make contacts within your community, either through the Chamber of Commerce, or other resources, to locate "Executives on Loan" or the "SCORE" program, which may be able to help you with staff development. Service clubs also may have these listings.

RSVP (Retired Service Volunteer Program) is another effective resource. Coordinate with other organizations and agencies to do programs cooperatively or swap trainers among your own organizations.

Suggested Readings

Library Specific

Avery, Elizabeth. *Staff Development*. Chicago, IL: Library Administration and Management Association, 2001.

Bessler, Joanne M. *Putting Service in Library Staff Training: A Patron-Centered Guide*. Chicago: American Library Association, 1994.

Brine, Alan. *Handbook for Library Training Practice and Development*. London: Applegate Publishing Company, 2009.

Caputo, Janette. *Stress and Burnout in Library Service*. Phoenix, AZ: Oryx, 1991.

Castelyn, Mary. *Promoting Excellence: Personal Management and Staff Development in Libraries*. New Providence, NJ: Saturn, 1992.

Donovan, Georgie L., and Miguel A. Figueroa. *Staff Development Strategies That Work! Stories and Strategies from New Librarians*. New York: Neal-Schuman, 2009.

Ensher, Ellen A., and Susan E. Murphy. *Power Mentoring: How Successful Mentors and Protégés Get the Most out of Their Relationship*. San Francisco, CA: Jossey-Bass, 2005.

Evans, G. Edward. *Performance Management and Appraisal: A How-To-Do-It Manual for Librarians*. New York: Neal-Schuman, 2004.

Gerding, Stephanie. *The Accidental Technology: A Guide for Libraries*. Medford, NJ: Information Today, 2007.

Glennan, Barbara. *Survey on Staff Development Policies*. Buffalo, NY: William S. Hein, 2007.

Massis, Bruce. *The Challenges of Library Learning: Solutions for Librarians*. New York: Routledge, 2008.

Rubin, Richard. *Human Resource Management in Libraries*. New York: Neal-Schuman, 1991.

Todaro, Julie, and Mark L. Smith. *Training Library Staff and Volunteers to Provide Extraordinary Customer Service*. New York: Neal-Schuman Publishers, 2006.

Stueart, Robert, and Barbara Moran. *Library Management, 5th Edition*. Littleton, CO: Libraries Unlimited, 1998.

Management and Business Oriented

Although we can learn from one another in the profession, it is equally important that we take advantage of the tremendous amount of material that has been developed for other nonprofits and for business. The advice and techniques that are included in these sources can easily be adapted to suit the particular needs of your library. I would not be surprised to learn that your collection includes many of these.

Allen, Kathleen. *Time and Information Management That Really Works!* Lincolnwood, IL: NTC Business Books, 1995.

Bailey, Gerald. *One Hundred One Activities for Creating Effective Technology Staff Development*. New York: Scholastic, 1994.

Brew, Angela. *Directions in Staff Development*. Houston, TX: Open U Press, 1995.

Drucker, Peter. *Managing for the Future*. New York: Penguin Group, 1992.

Frank, Milo. *How to Run a Successful Meeting—In Half the Time*. New York: Simon and Schuster, 1989.

Kirby, Tess. *The Can-Do Manager*. New York: American Management Association, 1989.

Klabnick, Joan. *Rewarding and Recognizing Employees: Ideas for Individuals, Teams, and Mangers*. New York: Irwin, 1995.

Lawrence, C. Edward. *How to Handle Staff Misconduct*. New York: Carwin, 1995.

Lockwood, Fred. *How to Present and Evaluate Flexible Learning Materials*. London: Kogan, 1995.

Mullins, Terry. *Staff Development Programs: A Guide to Evaluation*. New York: Carwin, 1994.

Rodriguez, Lori. *Manual of Staff Development*. New York: Mosby, 1995.

Stevens, Nicola. *Learning to Coach*. New York: How-To Books, 2009.

Tools for Trainers and Recognition Resources

Career Track Seminars on Tape
MS2 3083 Center Green Drive
Boulder, CO 80301-5408

In addition to sponsoring seminars, this company distributes both video and audio on a broad range of training topics.

Dinn Brothers Recognition Awards
68 Winter Street
Holyoke, MA 01041-9981

This is a collection of materials that can be used to increase productivity and improve safety as well as recognize success.

Motivation!
720 International Parkway
P.O. Box 450939
Sunrise, FL 33345-0939

This offers a collection of items that can be used to boost morale.

Index

About the Author

Marcia Trotta retired as Director of the Meriden, Connecticut, Public Library. She is currently a consultant and the adult program coordinator of the Connecticut Humanities Council.

Trotta is past president of the Connecticut Library Association, and was honored twice by them as the Outstanding Librarian. She is the author of *Managing Library Outreach Programs*, *Successful Staff Development*, and *Supervising Staff*, and the co-author of *The Librarian's Facility Management Handbook*, all for Neal-Schuman.